I0605898

GRAPHIC LIBRARY ™

GRAPHIC EXPEDITIONS

SEARCHING FOR

UFOs

AN Isabel Soto INVESTIGATION

by Aaron Sautter
illustrated by Cynthia Martin and Barbara Schulz

Consultant:
Jerome Clark, Editor
International UFO Reporter
J. Allen Hynek Center for UFO Studies
Chicago, Illinois

CAPSTONE PRESS
a capstone imprint

Graphic Library is published by Capstone Press,
151 Good Counsel Drive, P.O. Box 669, Mankato, Minnesota 56002.
www.capstonepress.com

Printed in the United States of America in Stevens Point, Wisconsin.

092009
005619WZS10

Books published by Capstone Press are manufactured with paper containing at least 10 percent post-consumer waste.

Library of Congress Cataloging-in-Publication Data
Sautter, Aaron.
Searching for UFOs : an Isabel Soto investigation / by Aaron Sautter ; illustrated by Cynthia Martin and Barbara Schulz.
p. cm. — (Graphic library. Graphic expeditions)
Includes bibliographical references and index.
Summary: "In graphic novel format, follows the adventures of Isabel Soto as she investigates UFOs" — Provided by publisher.
ISBN 978-1-4296-3974-3 (library binding)
ISBN 978-1-4296-4859-2 (paperback)
1. Unidentified flying objects — Comic books, strips, etc. — Juvenile literature. 2. Graphic novels. I. Martin, Cynthia, 1961– ill. II. Schulz, Barbara (Barbara Jo), ill. III. Title.
TL789.2.S28 2010
001.942 — dc22 2009026659

Designer
Alison Thiele

Media Researcher
Wanda Winch

Cover Artist
Tod G. Smith

Production Specialist
Laura Manthe

Colorist
Krista Ward

Editor
Christopher L. Harbo

Photo Credits: CORBIS/Bettmann, 25; Fortean Picture Library, 15; iStockphoto/Joze Pojbic, 19

Design Elements: Shutterstock/Chen Ping Hung (framed edge design); mmmm (world map design); Mushakesa (abstract lines design); Najin (old parchment design)

TABLE of CONTENTS

CHAPTER 1 | BLAST IN THE PAST

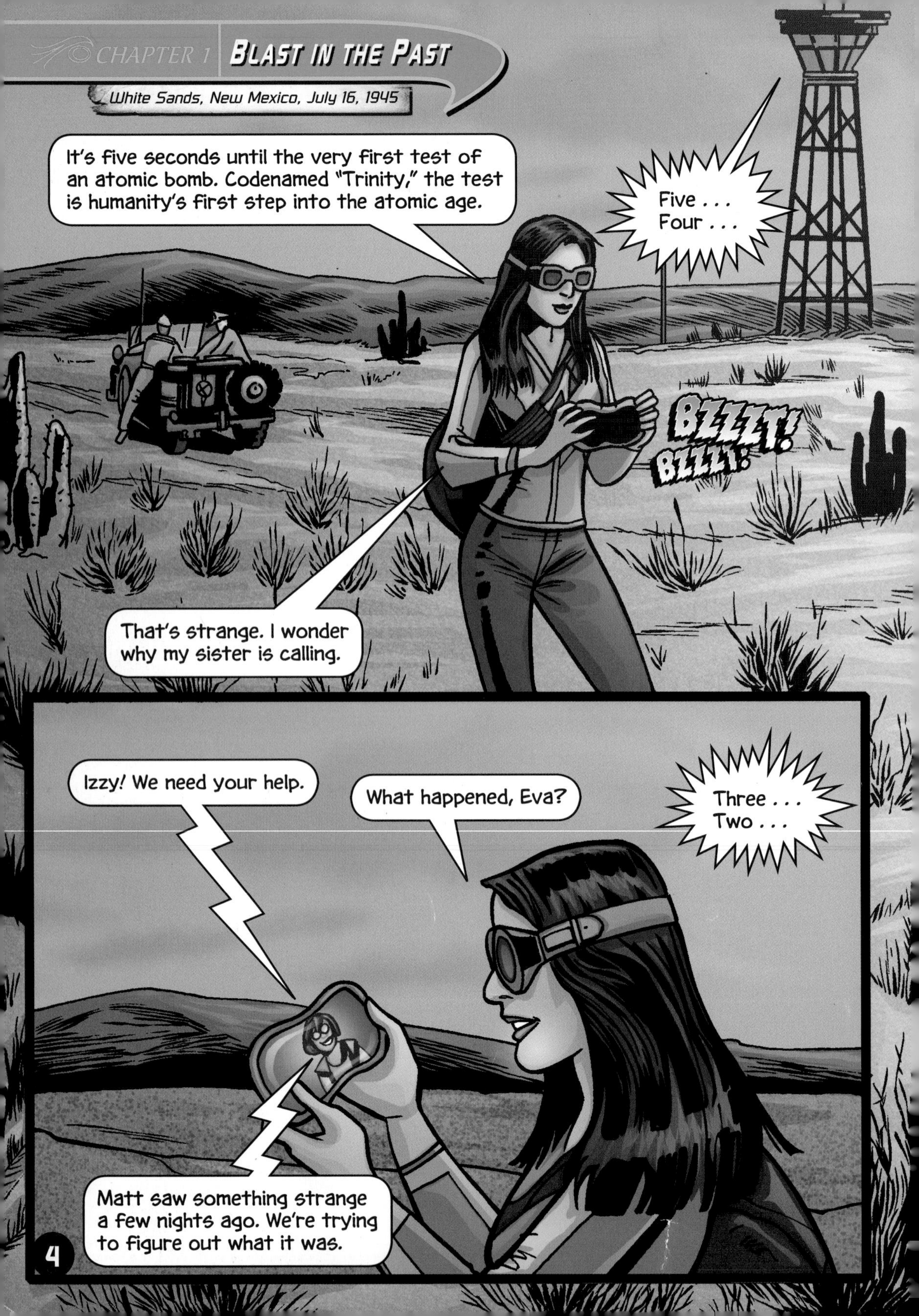
White Sands, New Mexico, July 16, 1945
It's five seconds until the very first test of an atomic bomb. Codenamed "Trinity," the test is humanity's first step into the atomic age.
Five . . . Four . . .
BZZZT! BZZZT!
That's strange. I wonder why my sister is calling.
Izzy! We need your help.
What happened, Eva?
Three . . . Two . . .
Matt saw something strange a few nights ago. We're trying to figure out what it was.

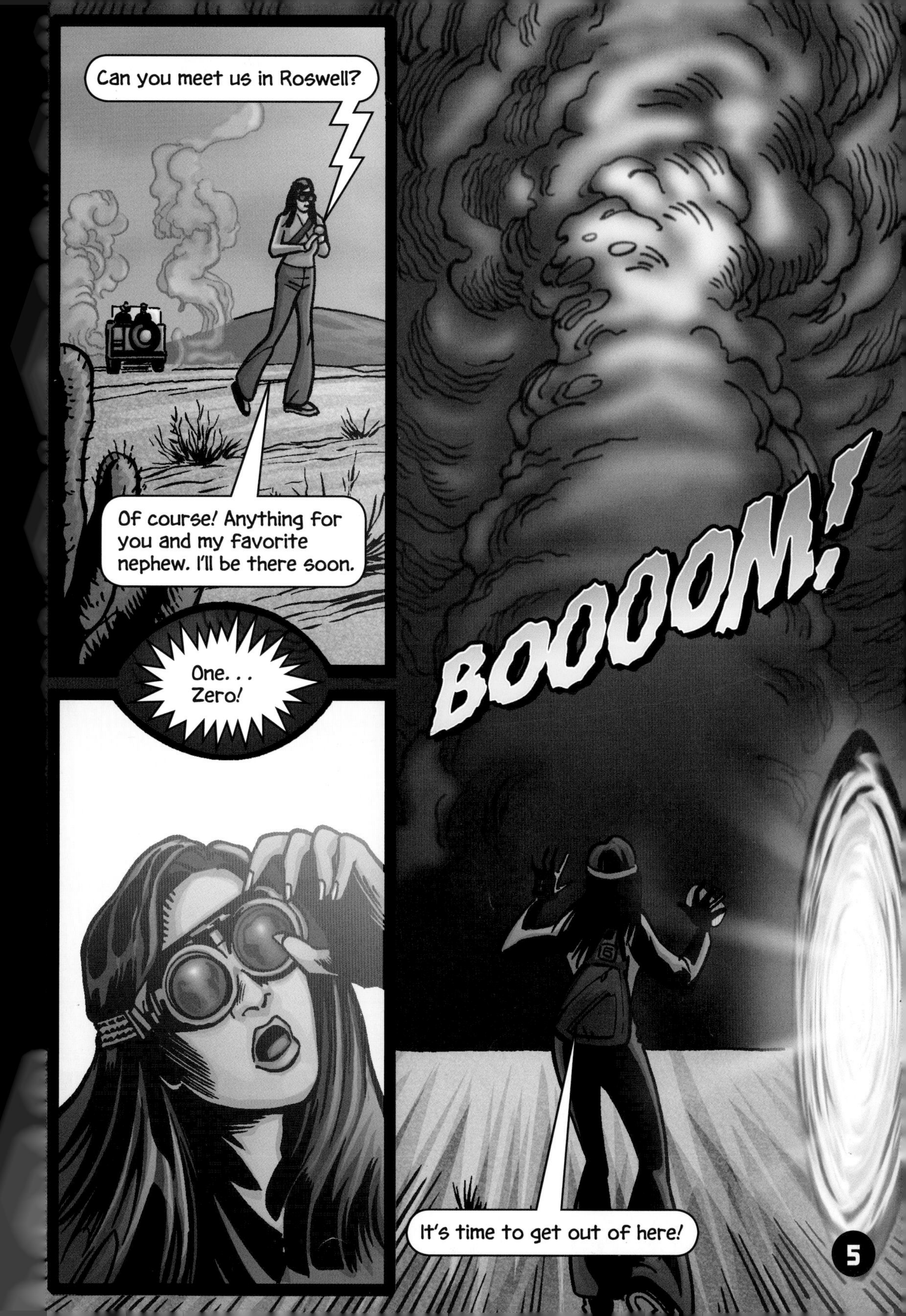

Can you meet us in Roswell?
Of course! Anything for you and my favorite nephew. I'll be there soon.
One. . . Zero!
BOOOOM!
It's time to get out of here!

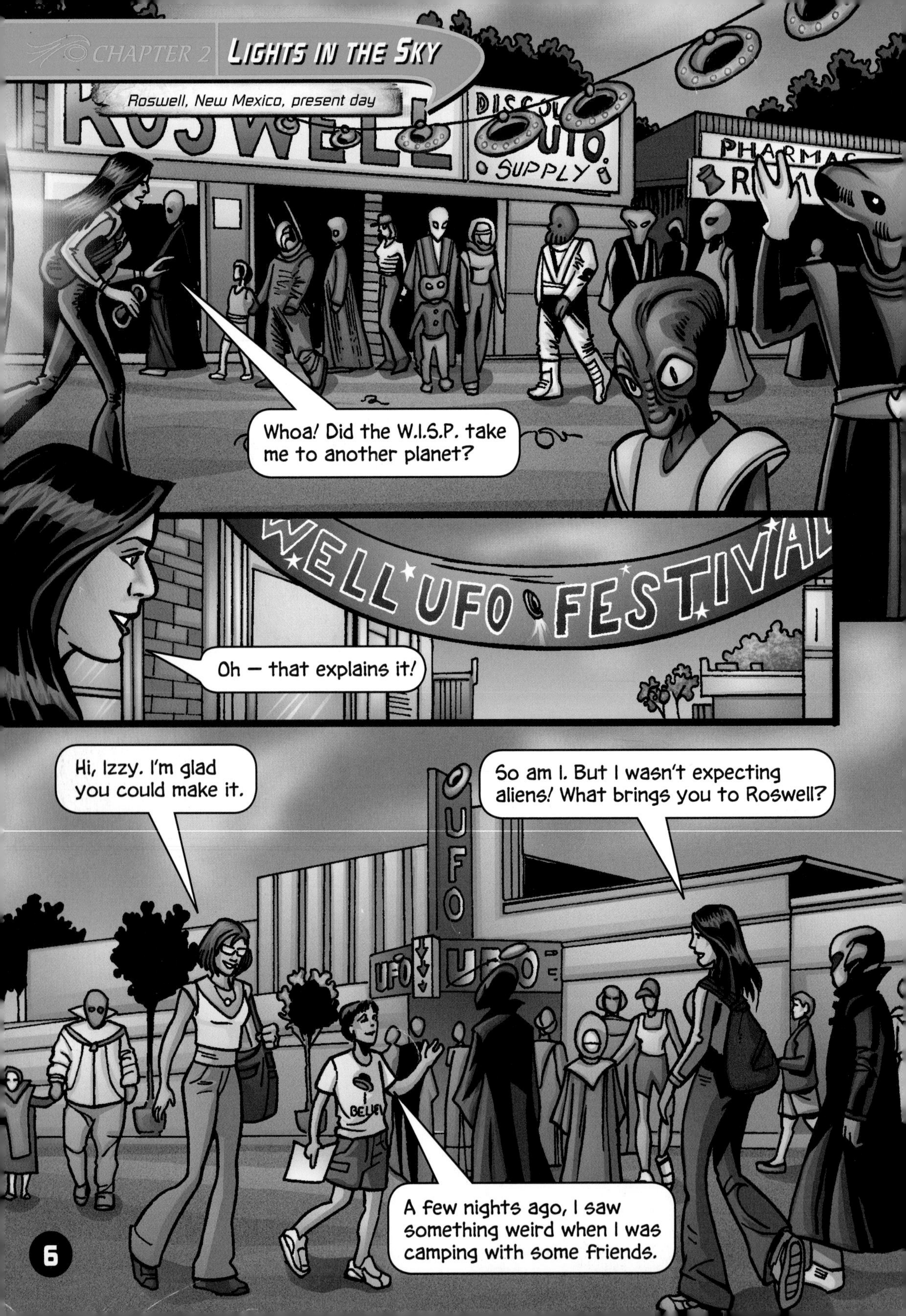
CHAPTER 2 LIGHTS IN THE SKY
Roswell, New Mexico, present day
Whoa! Did the W.I.S.P. take me to another planet?
Oh — that explains it!
Hi, Izzy. I'm glad you could make it.
So am I. But I wasn't expecting aliens! What brings you to Roswell?
A few nights ago, I saw something weird when I was camping with some friends.

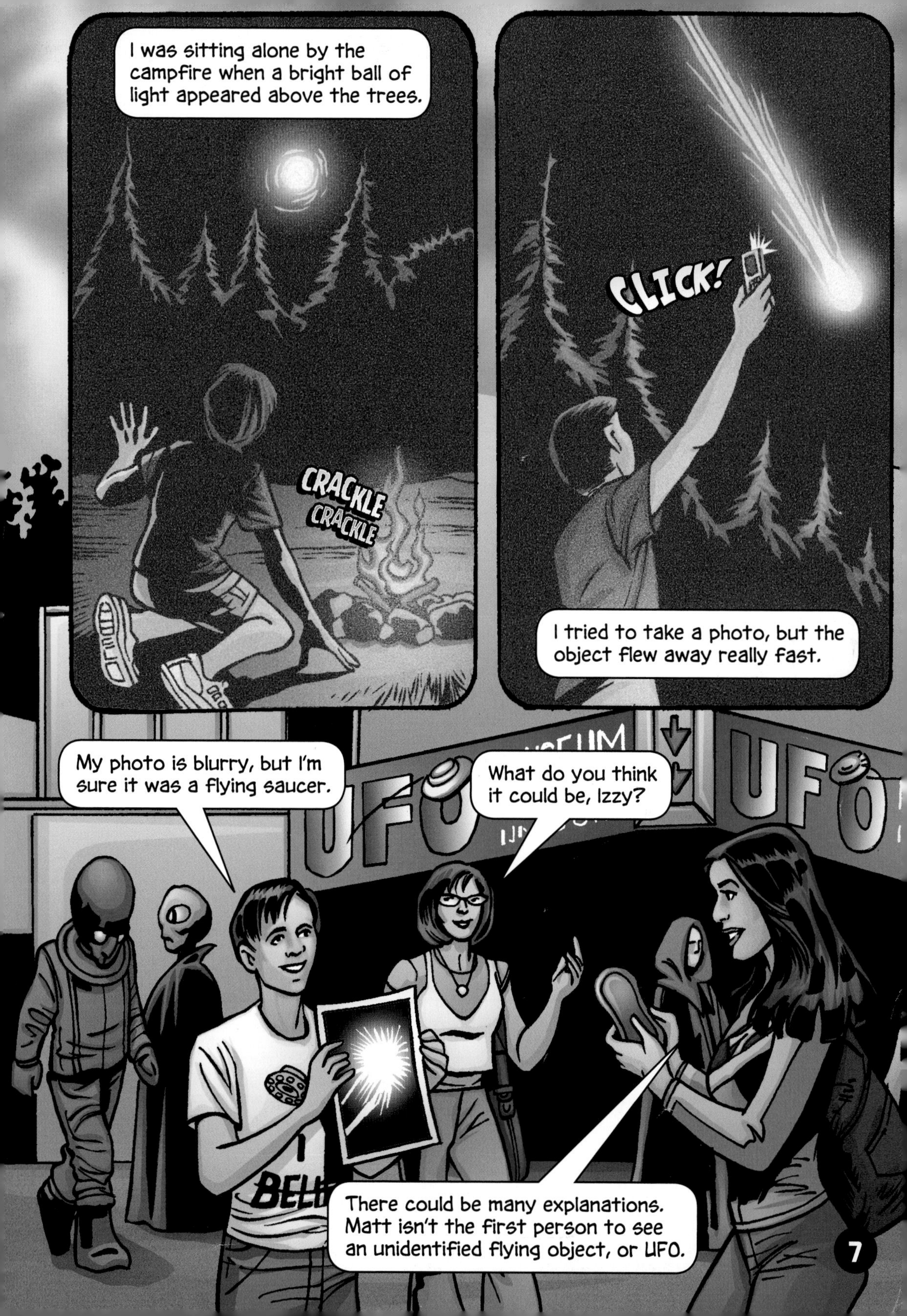
I was sitting alone by the campfire when a bright ball of light appeared above the trees.
CRACKLE CRACKLE
CLICK!
I tried to take a photo, but the object flew away really fast.
My photo is blurry, but I'm sure it was a flying saucer.
What do you think it could be, Izzy?
UFO
There could be many explanations. Matt isn't the first person to see an unidentified flying object, or UFO.

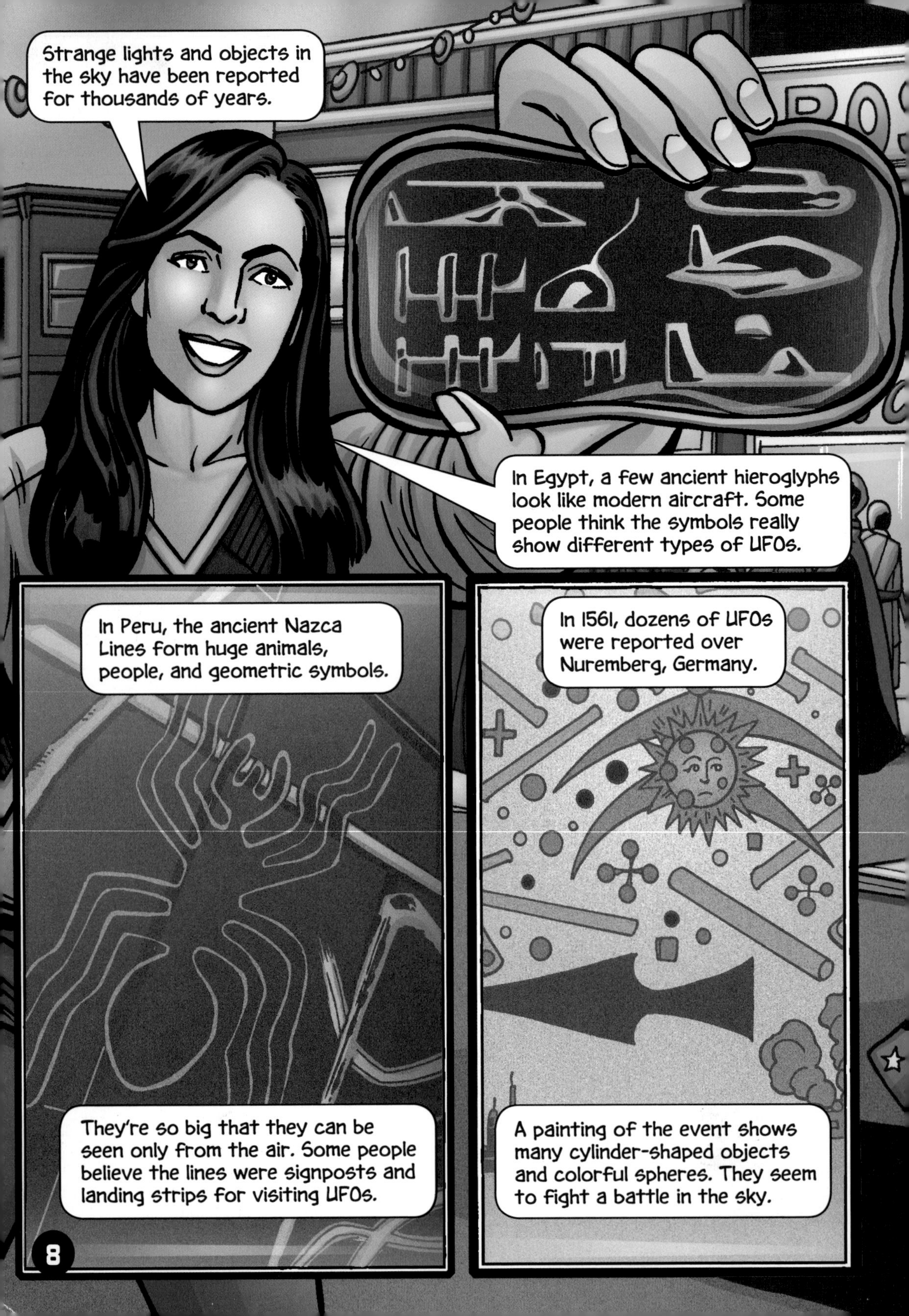
Strange lights and objects in the sky have been reported for thousands of years.
In Egypt, a few ancient hieroglyphs look like modern aircraft. Some people think the symbols really show different types of UFOs.
In Peru, the ancient Nazca Lines form huge animals, people, and geometric symbols.
They're so big that they can be seen only from the air. Some people believe the lines were signposts and landing strips for visiting UFOs.
In 1561, dozens of UFOs were reported over Nuremberg, Germany.
A painting of the event shows many cylinder-shaped objects and colorful spheres. They seem to fight a battle in the sky.

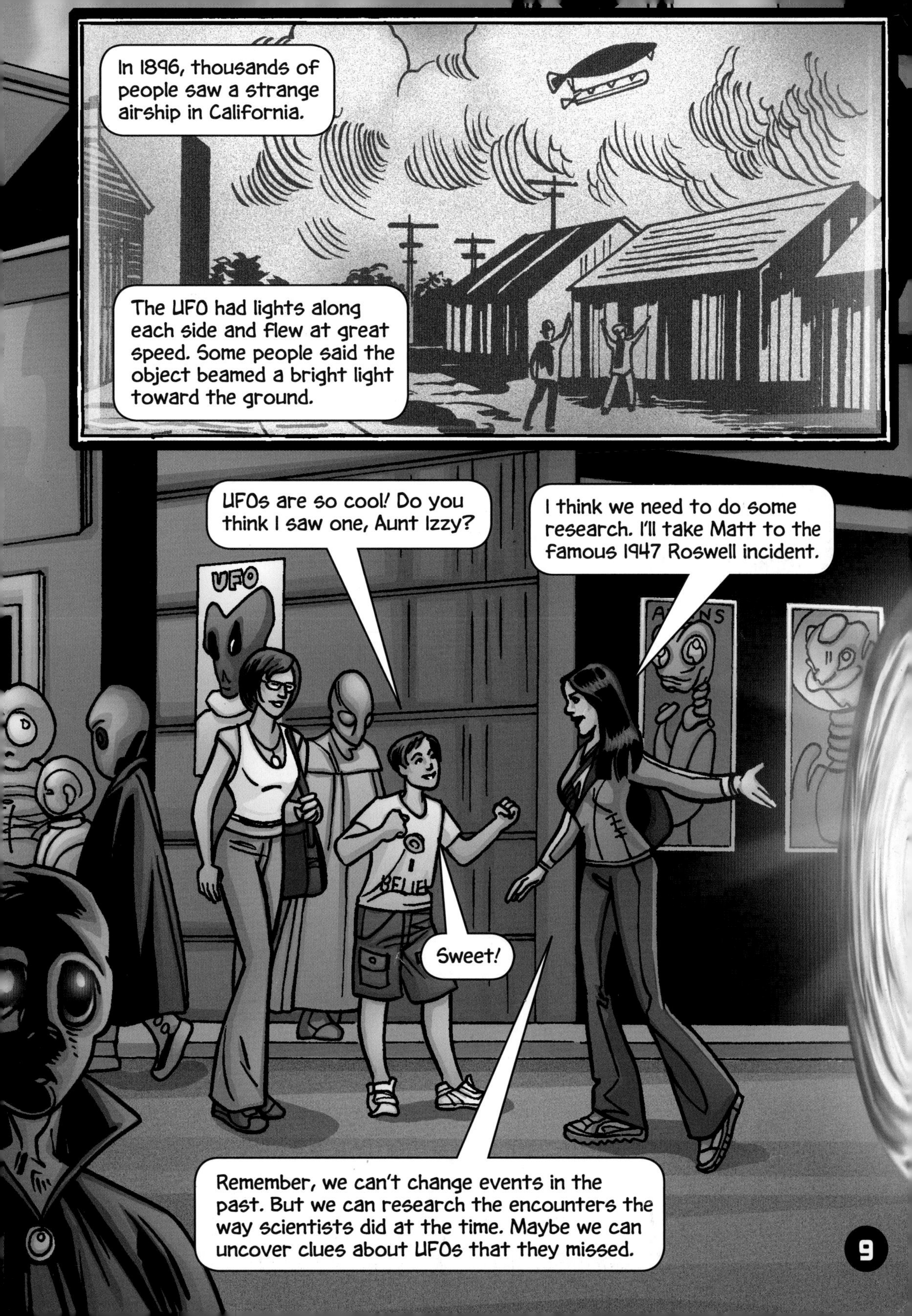
In 1896, thousands of people saw a strange airship in California.
The UFO had lights along each side and flew at great speed. Some people said the object beamed a bright light toward the ground.
UFOs are so cool! Do you think I saw one, Aunt Izzy?
I think we need to do some research. I'll take Matt to the famous 1947 Roswell incident.
UFO
Sweet!
Remember, we can't change events in the past. But we can research the encounters the way scientists did at the time. Maybe we can uncover clues about UFOs that they missed.

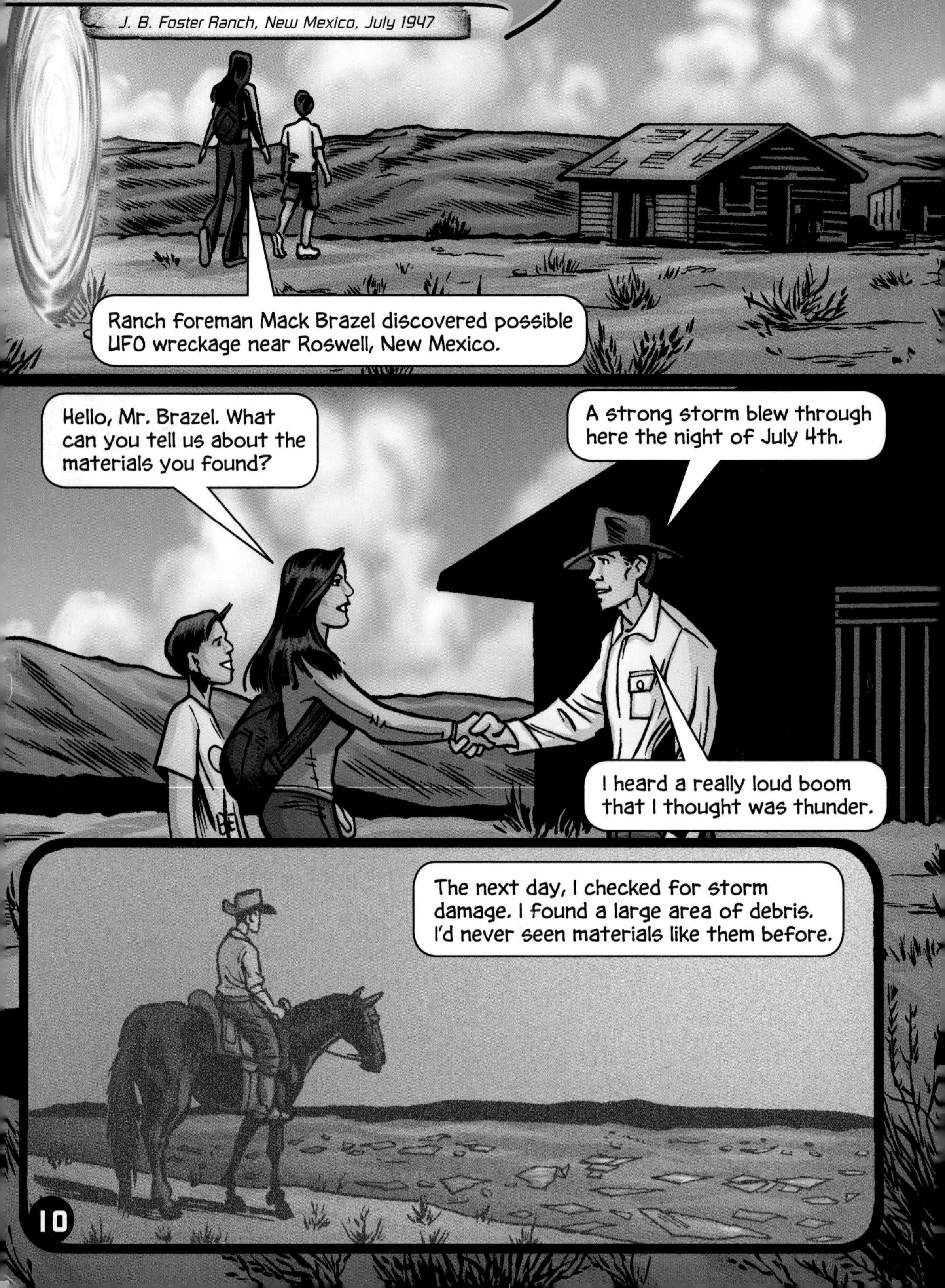
J. B. Foster Ranch, New Mexico, July 1947
Ranch foreman Mack Brazel discovered possible UFO wreckage near Roswell, New Mexico.
Hello, Mr. Brazel. What can you tell us about the materials you found?
A strong storm blew through here the night of July 4th.
I heard a really loud boom that I thought was thunder.
The next day, I checked for storm damage. I found a large area of debris. I'd never seen materials like them before.

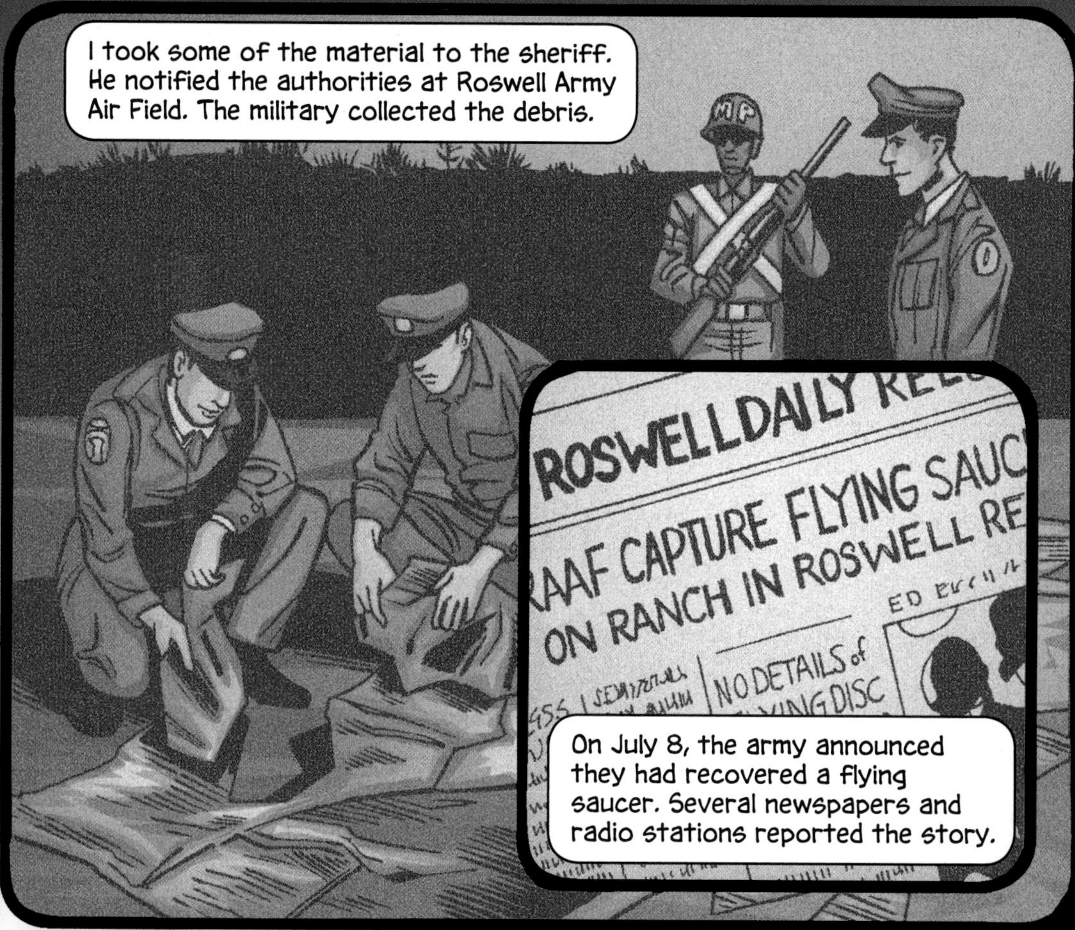
I took some of the material to the sheriff. He notified the authorities at Roswell Army Air Field. The military collected the debris.
ROSWELL DAILY
CAPTURE FLYING
ON RANCH IN ROSWELL
NO DETAILS of
On July 8, the army announced they had recovered a flying saucer. Several newspapers and radio stations reported the story.

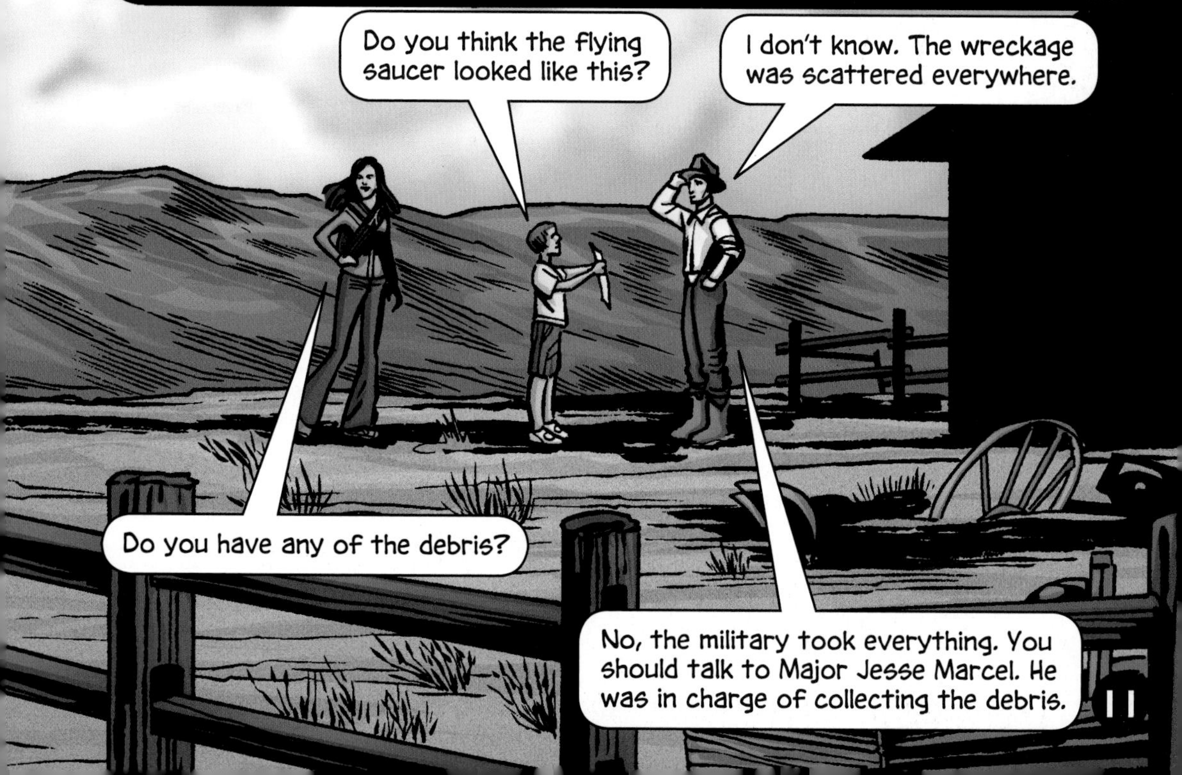
Do you think the flying saucer looked like this?
I don't know. The wreckage was scattered everywhere.
Do you have any of the debris?
No, the military took everything. You should talk to Major Jesse Marcel. He was in charge of collecting the debris.

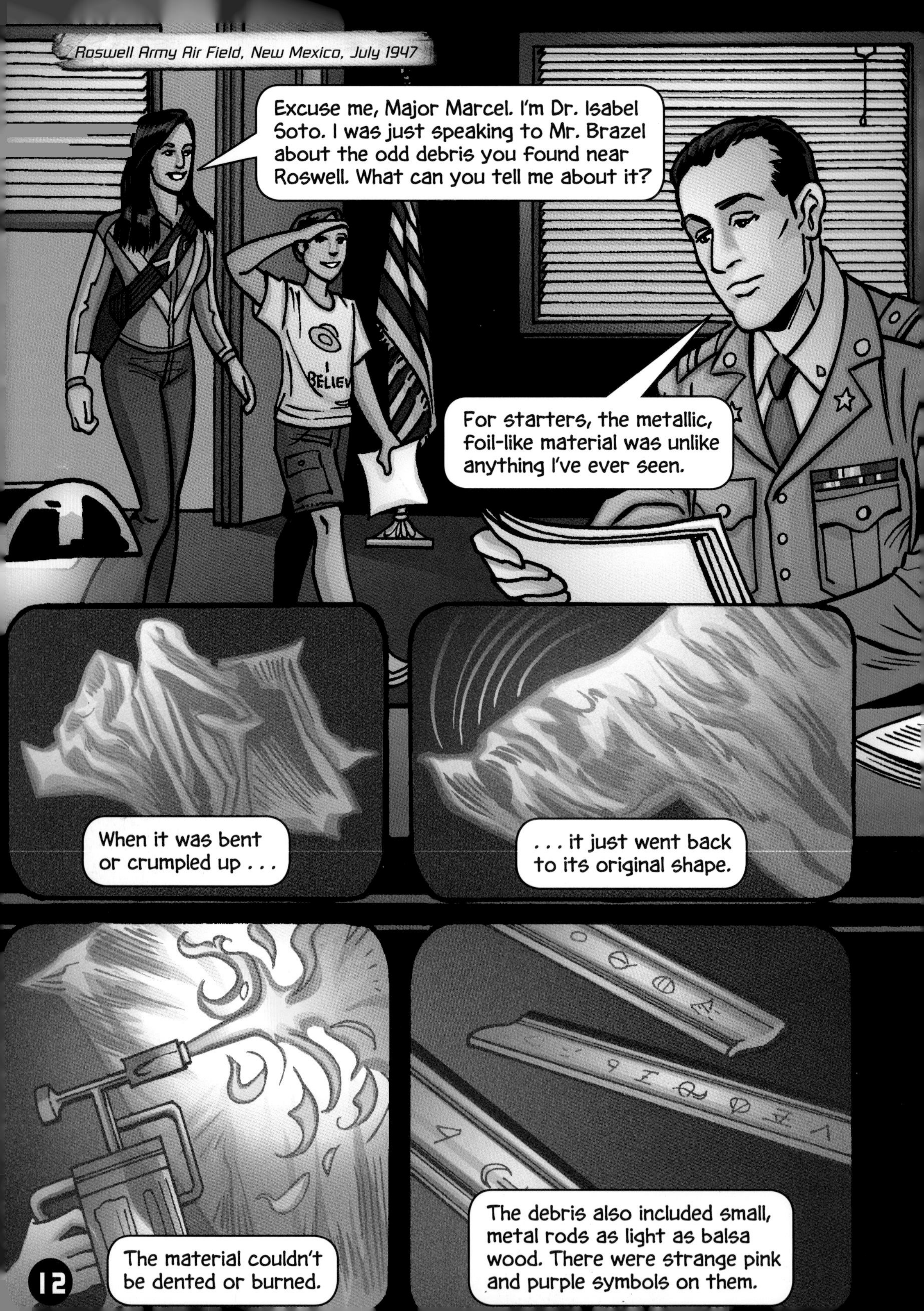
Roswell Army Air Field, New Mexico, July 1947
Excuse me, Major Marcel. I'm Dr. Isabel Soto. I was just speaking to Mr. Brazel about the odd debris you found near Roswell. What can you tell me about it?
I BELIEVE
For starters, the metallic, foil-like material was unlike anything I've ever seen.
When it was bent or crumpled up . . .
. . . it just went back to its original shape.
The material couldn't be dented or burned.
The debris also included small, metal rods as light as balsa wood. There were strange pink and purple symbols on them.

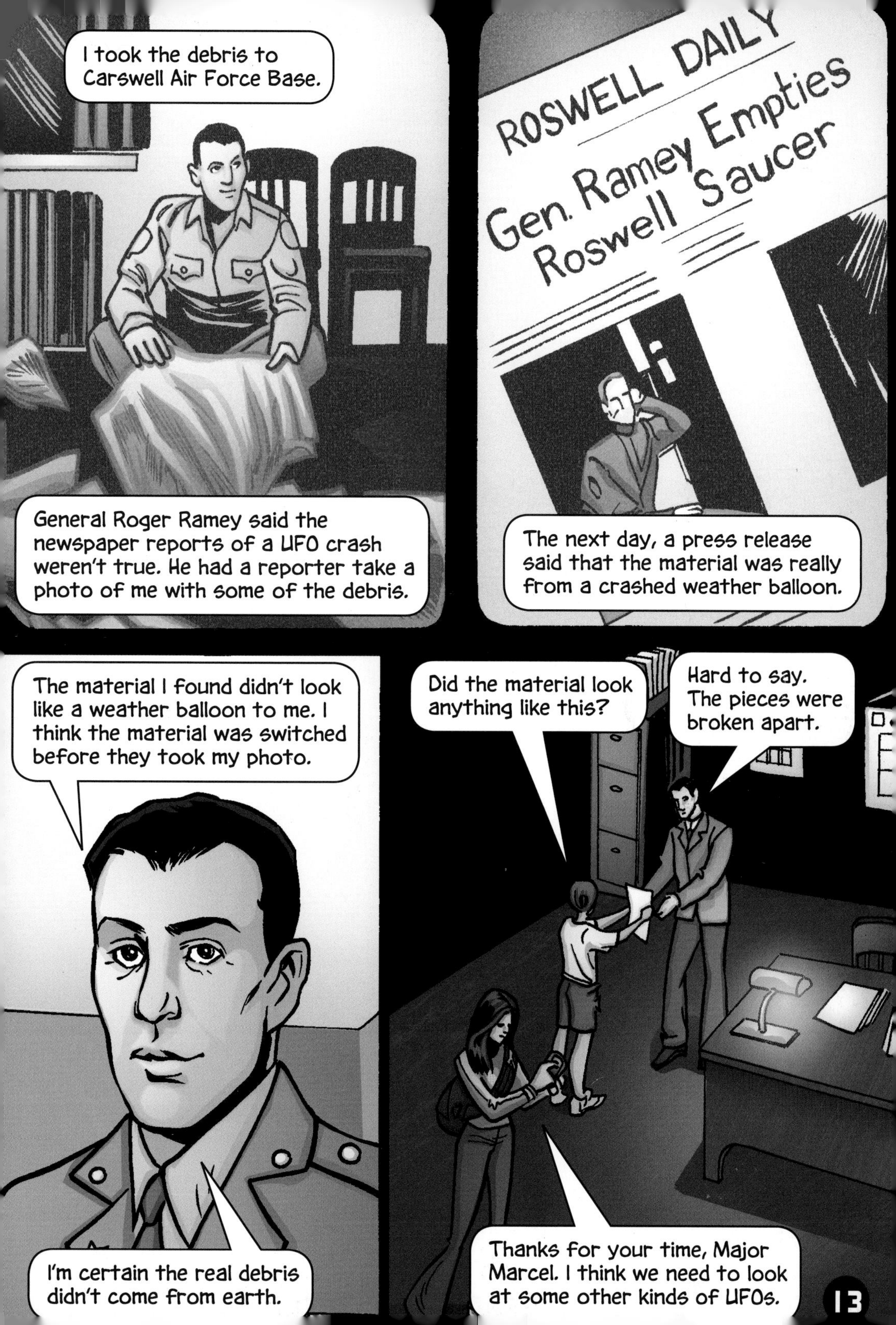
I took the debris to Carswell Air Force Base.
General Roger Ramey said the newspaper reports of a UFO crash weren't true. He had a reporter take a photo of me with some of the debris.
ROSWELL DAILY
Gen. Ramey Empties Roswell Saucer
The next day, a press release said that the material was really from a crashed weather balloon.
The material I found didn't look like a weather balloon to me. I think the material was switched before they took my photo.
I'm certain the real debris didn't come from earth.
Did the material look anything like this?
Hard to say. The pieces were broken apart.
Thanks for your time, Major Marcel. I think we need to look at some other kinds of UFOs.

CHAPTER 4 Close Encounters

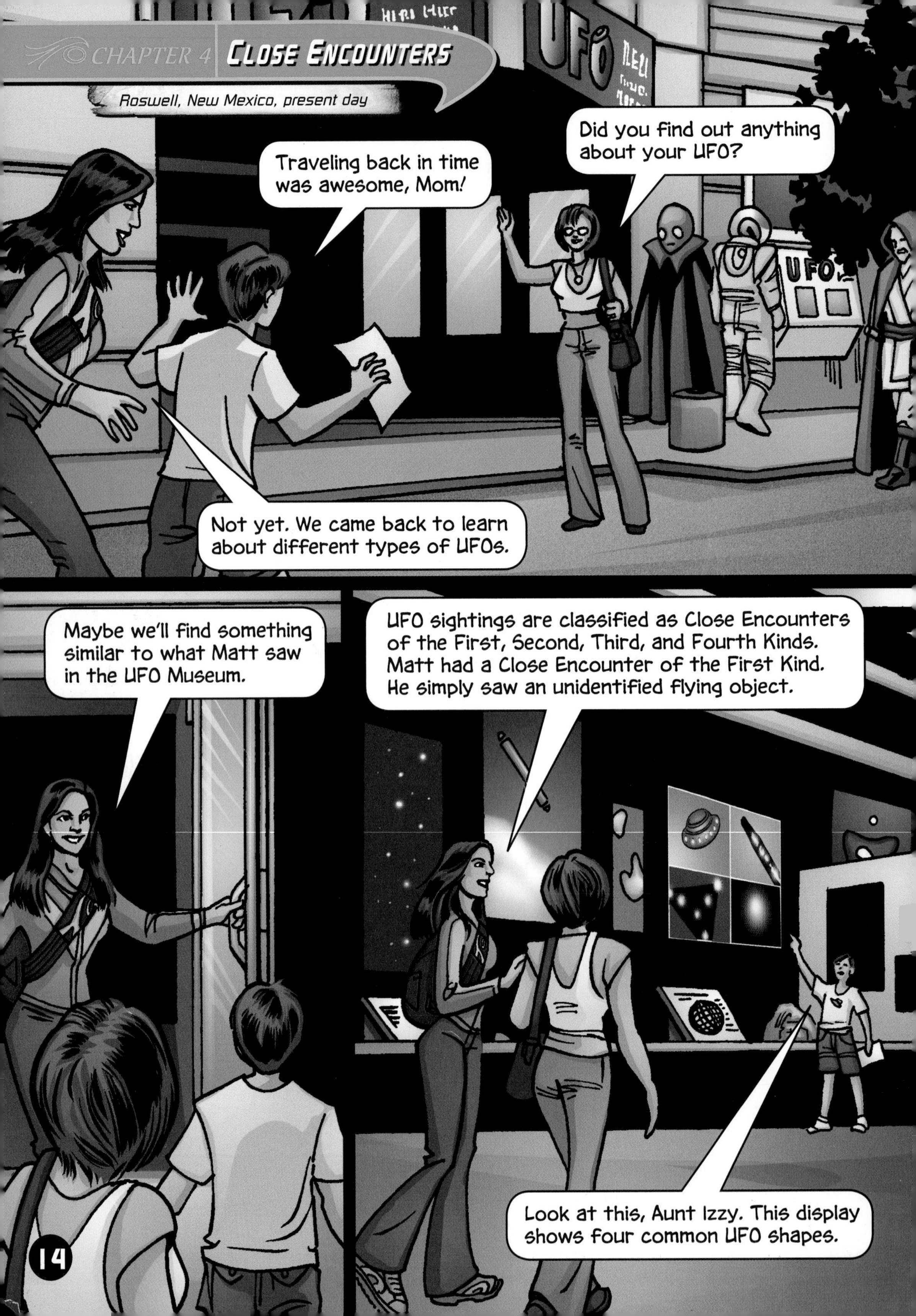

Roswell, New Mexico, present day
Traveling back in time was awesome, Mom!
Did you find out anything about your UFO?
Not yet. We came back to learn about different types of UFOs.
UFO
Maybe we'll find something similar to what Matt saw in the UFO Museum.
UFO sightings are classified as Close Encounters of the First, Second, Third, and Fourth Kinds. Matt had a Close Encounter of the First Kind. He simply saw an unidentified flying object.
Look at this, Aunt Izzy. This display shows four common UFO shapes.

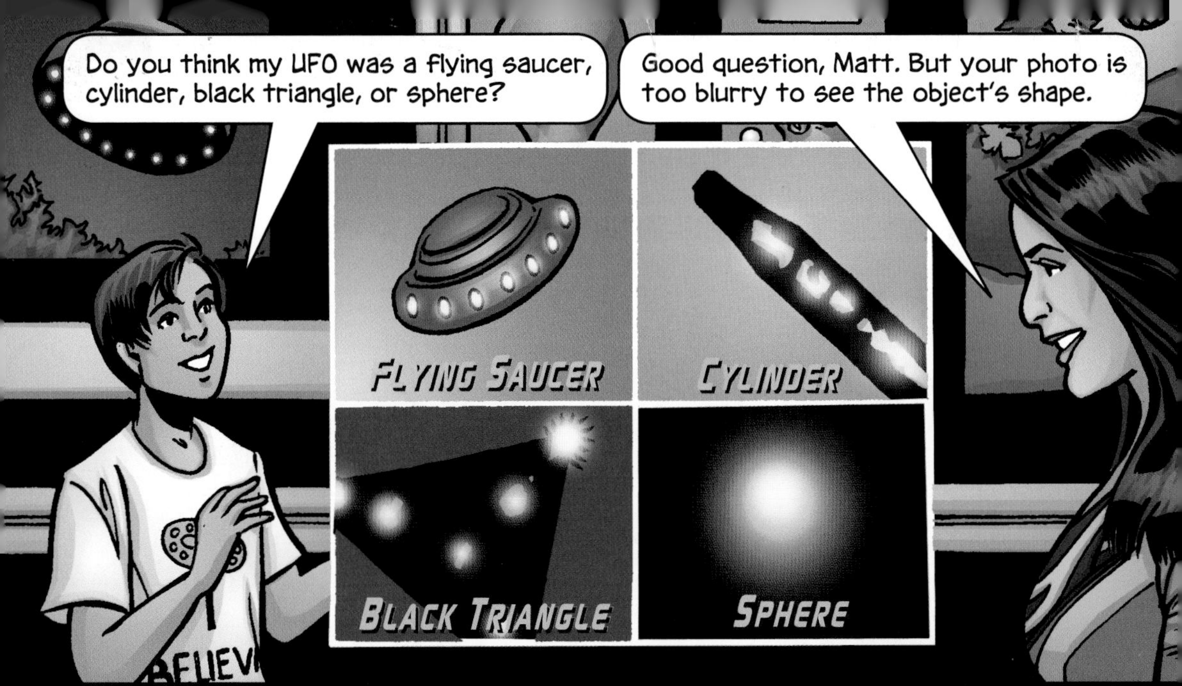
Do you think my UFO was a flying saucer, cylinder, black triangle, or sphere?
Good question, Matt. But your photo is too blurry to see the object's shape.
FLYING SAUCER
CYLINDER
BLACK TRIANGLE
SPHERE

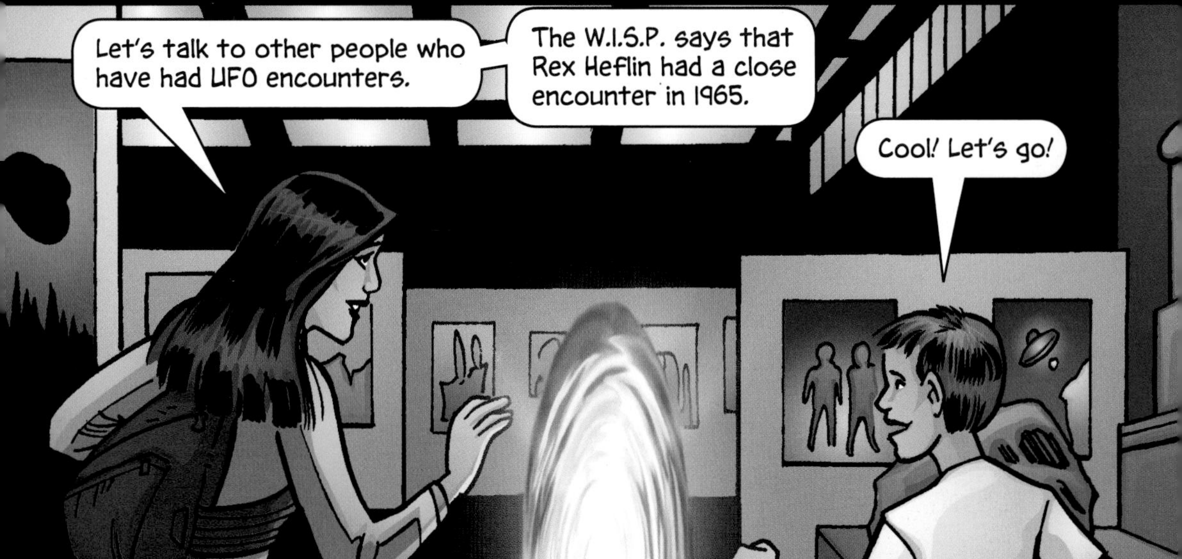
Let's talk to other people who have had UFO encounters.
The W.I.S.P. says that Rex Heflin had a close encounter in 1965.
Cool! Let's go!

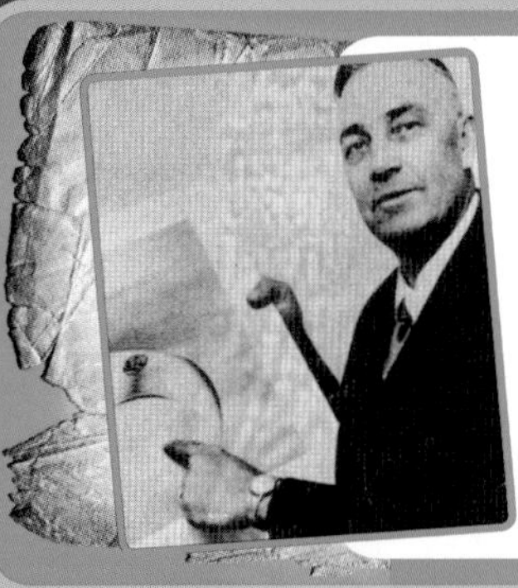

THE FIRST FLYING SAUCERS

On June 24, 1947, Kenneth Arnold was flying his small plane near Mount Rainier in Washington State. Suddenly he saw nine strange objects flying at fantastic speeds. Arnold said the objects flew "like a saucer would if you skip it across water." Newspapers started calling the objects "flying saucers." The term stuck.

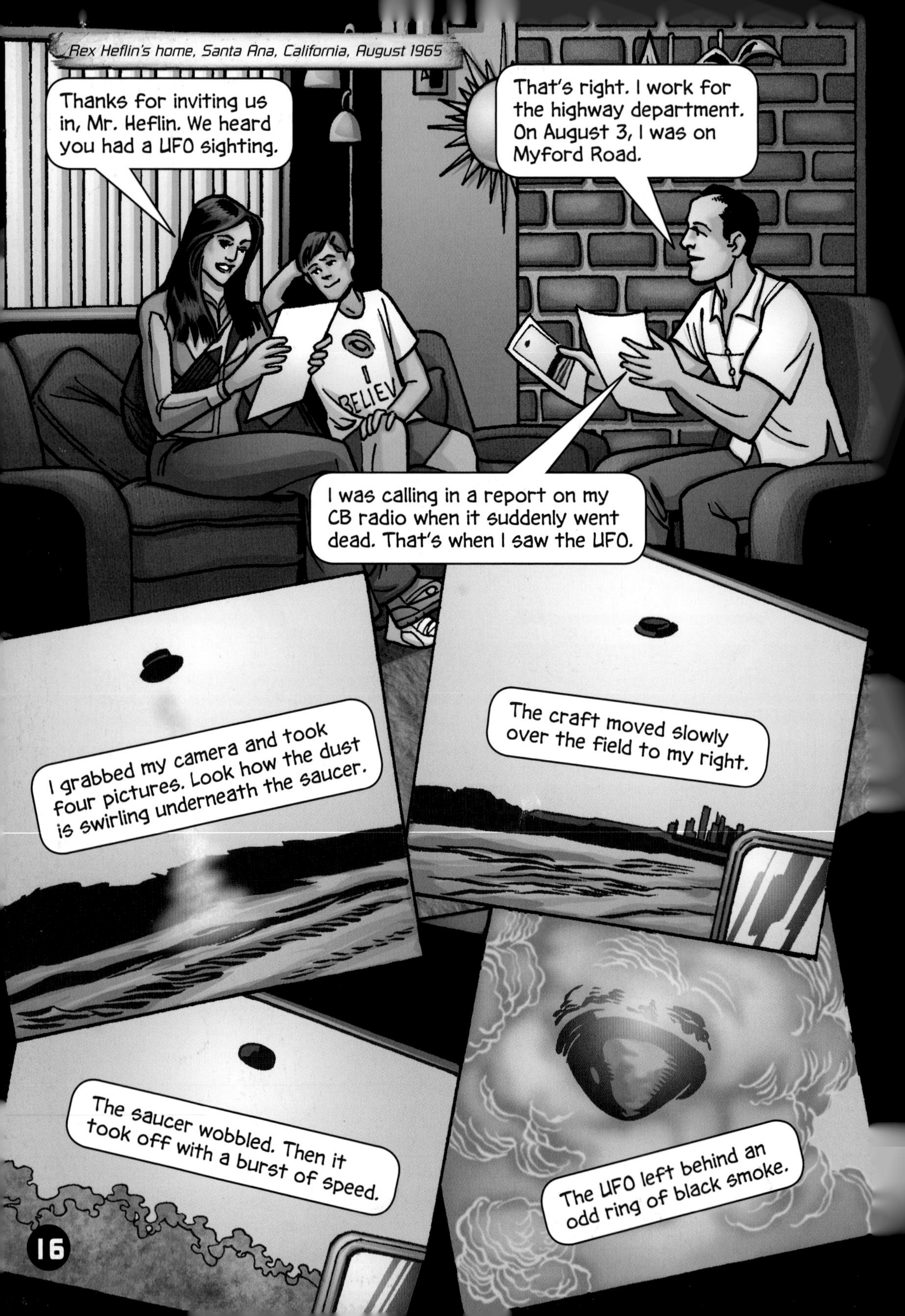

Rex Heflin's home, Santa Ana, California, August 1965
Thanks for inviting us in, Mr. Heflin. We heard you had a UFO sighting.
That's right. I work for the highway department. On August 3, I was on Myford Road.
I was calling in a report on my CB radio when it suddenly went dead. That's when I saw the UFO.
I grabbed my camera and took four pictures. Look how the dust is swirling underneath the saucer.
The craft moved slowly over the field to my right.
The saucer wobbled. Then it took off with a burst of speed.
The UFO left behind an odd ring of black smoke.

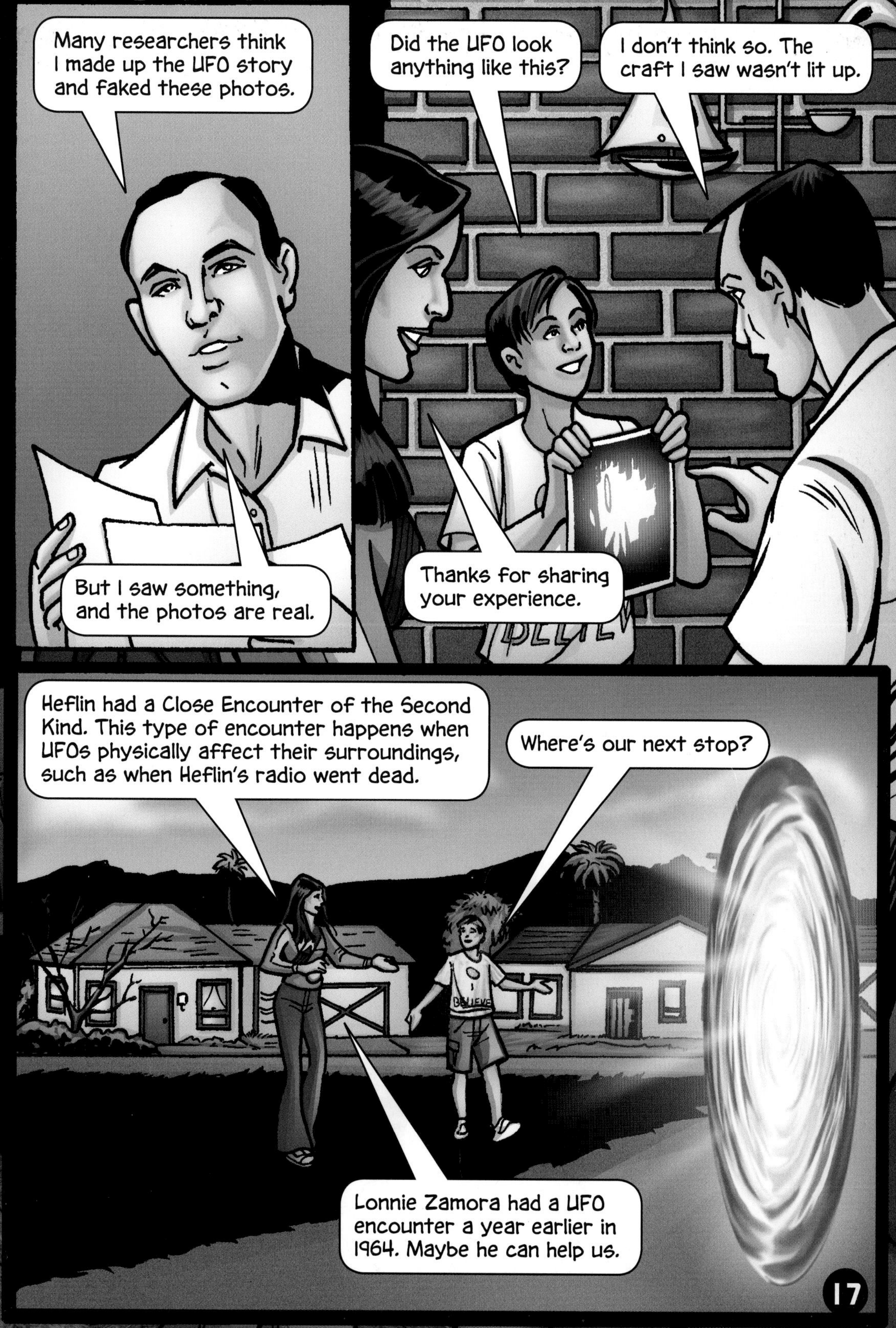

Many researchers think I made up the UFO story and faked these photos.
But I saw something, and the photos are real.
Did the UFO look anything like this?
I don't think so. The craft I saw wasn't lit up.
Thanks for sharing your experience.
Heflin had a Close Encounter of the Second Kind. This type of encounter happens when UFOs physically affect their surroundings, such as when Heflin's radio went dead.
Where's our next stop?
Lonnie Zamora had a UFO encounter a year earlier in 1964. Maybe he can help us.

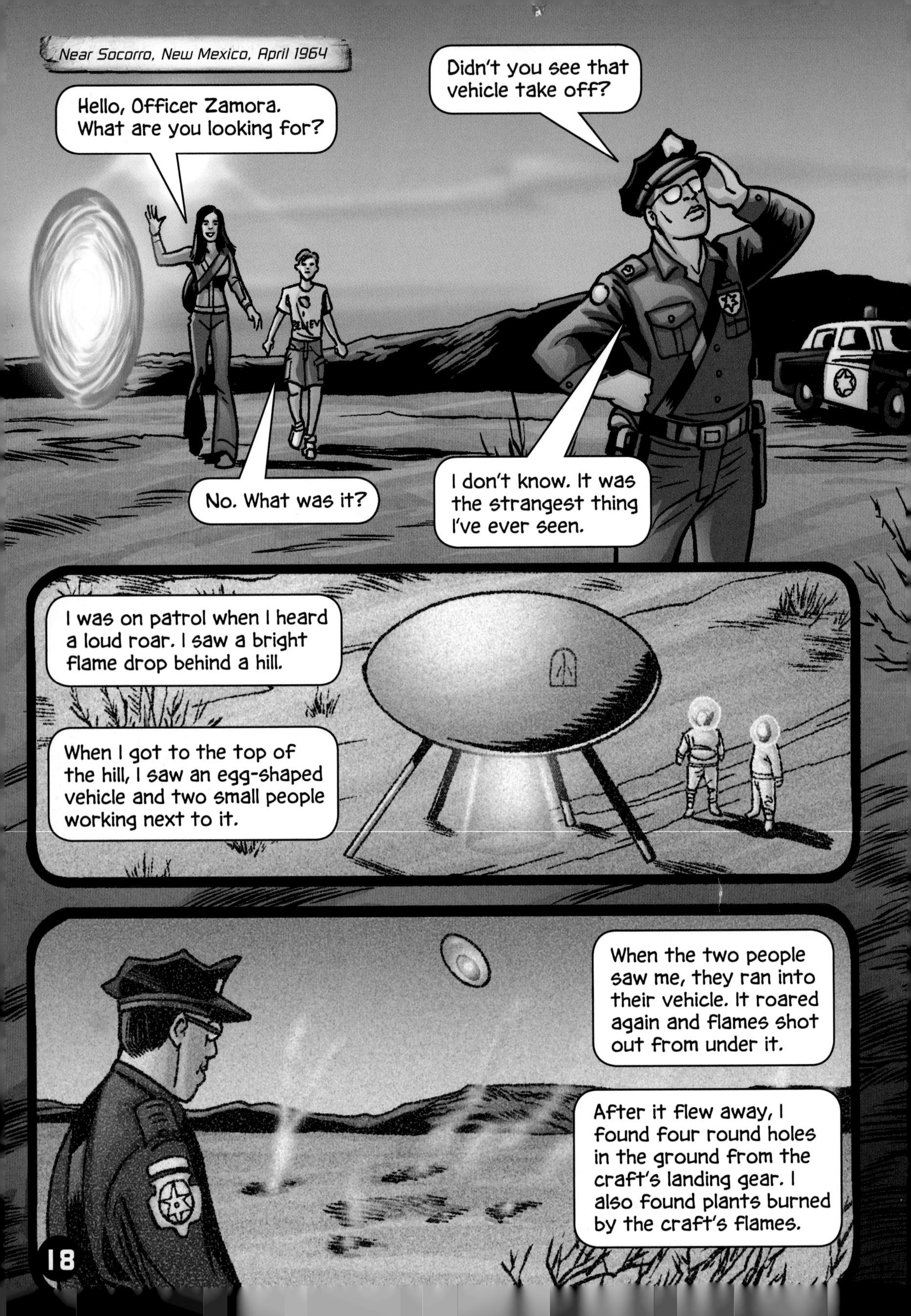
Near Socorro, New Mexico, April 1964
Hello, Officer Zamora. What are you looking for?
Didn't you see that vehicle take off?
No. What was it?
I don't know. It was the strangest thing I've ever seen.
I was on patrol when I heard a loud roar. I saw a bright flame drop behind a hill.
When I got to the top of the hill, I saw an egg-shaped vehicle and two small people working next to it.
When the two people saw me, they ran into their vehicle. It roared again and flames shot out from under it.
After it flew away, I found four round holes in the ground from the craft's landing gear. I also found plants burned by the craft's flames.

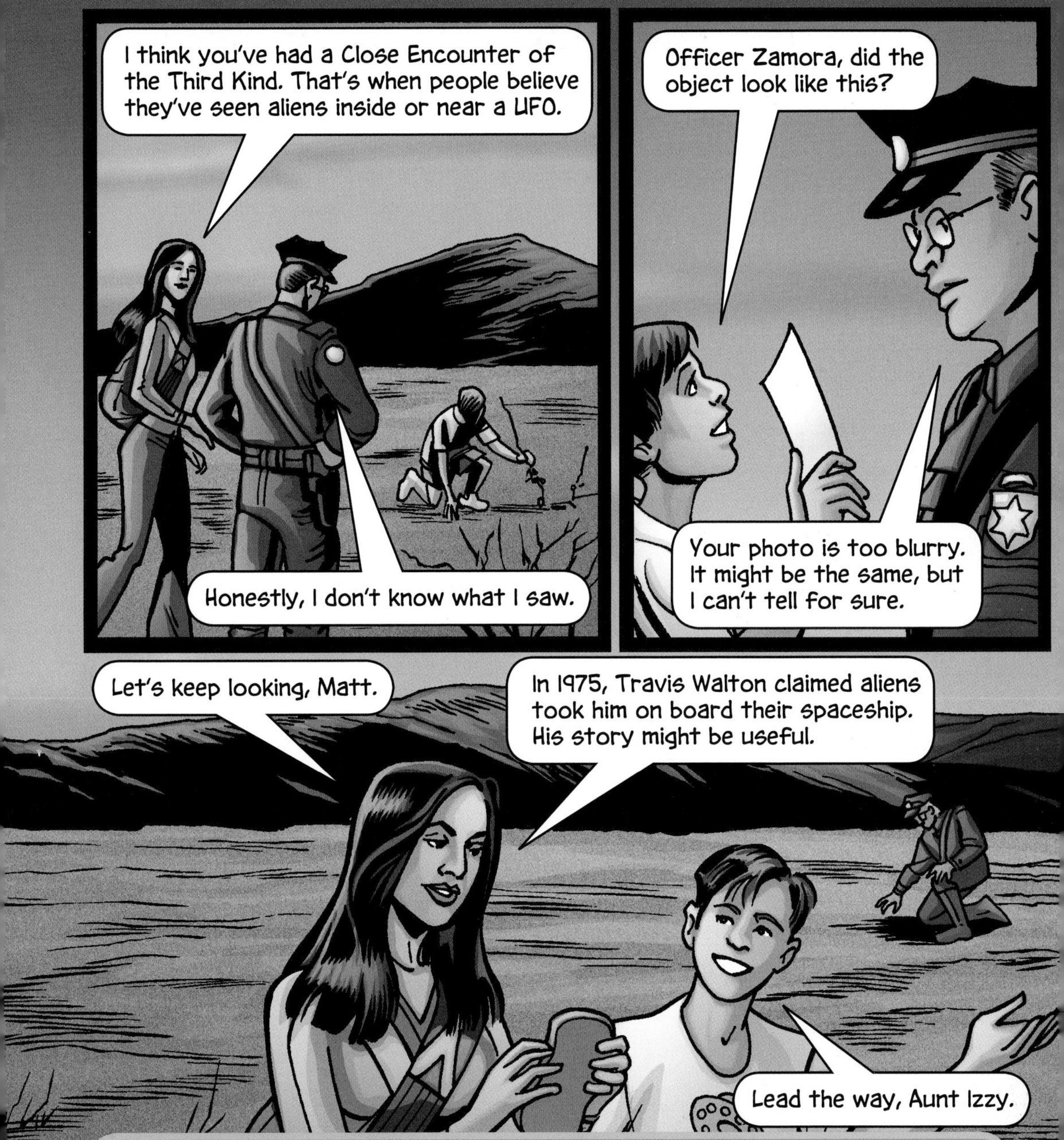
I think you've had a Close Encounter of the Third Kind. That's when people believe they've seen aliens inside or near a UFO.
Honestly, I don't know what I saw.
Officer Zamora, did the object look like this?
Your photo is too blurry. It might be the same, but I can't tell for sure.
Let's keep looking, Matt.
In 1975, Travis Walton claimed aliens took him on board their spaceship. His story might be useful.
Lead the way, Aunt Izzy.

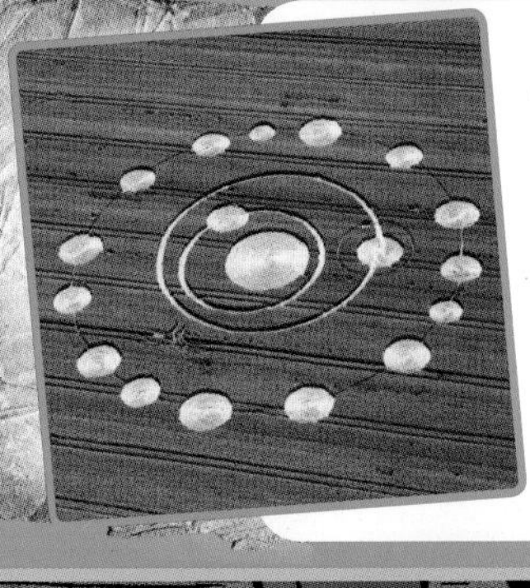

Crop Circles

Strange circles have appeared in fields for hundreds of years. Some people believe aliens made crop circles to communicate with humans. Many people claim that they've made crop circles as a practical joke. However, many circles seem too large and complicated for people to make in one night.

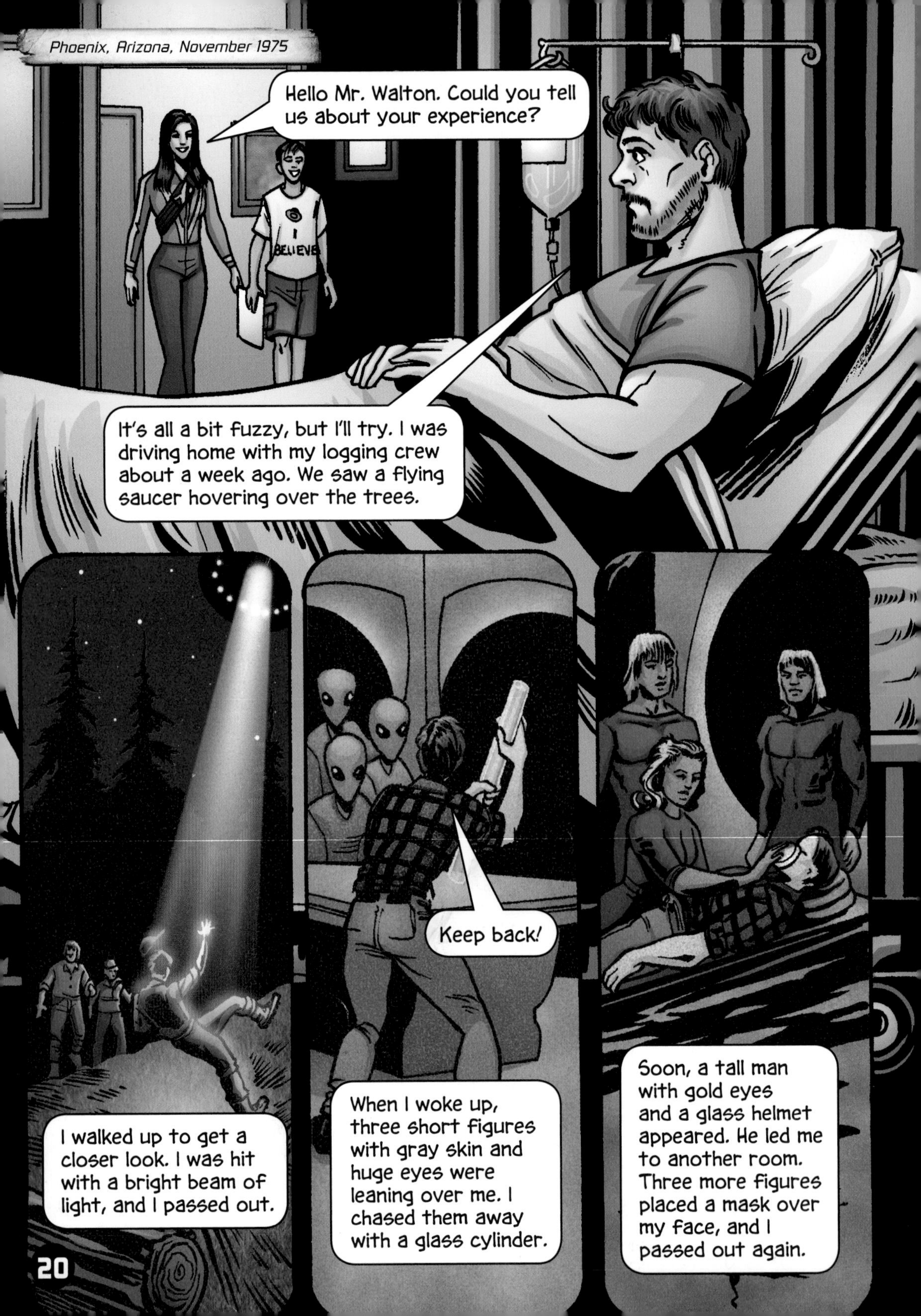

Phoenix, Arizona, November 1975
Hello Mr. Walton. Could you tell us about your experience?
I BELIEVE
It's all a bit fuzzy, but I'll try. I was driving home with my logging crew about a week ago. We saw a flying saucer hovering over the trees.
I walked up to get a closer look. I was hit with a bright beam of light, and I passed out.
Keep back!
When I woke up, three short figures with gray skin and huge eyes were leaning over me. I chased them away with a glass cylinder.
Soon, a tall man with gold eyes and a glass helmet appeared. He led me to another room. Three more figures placed a mask over my face, and I passed out again.

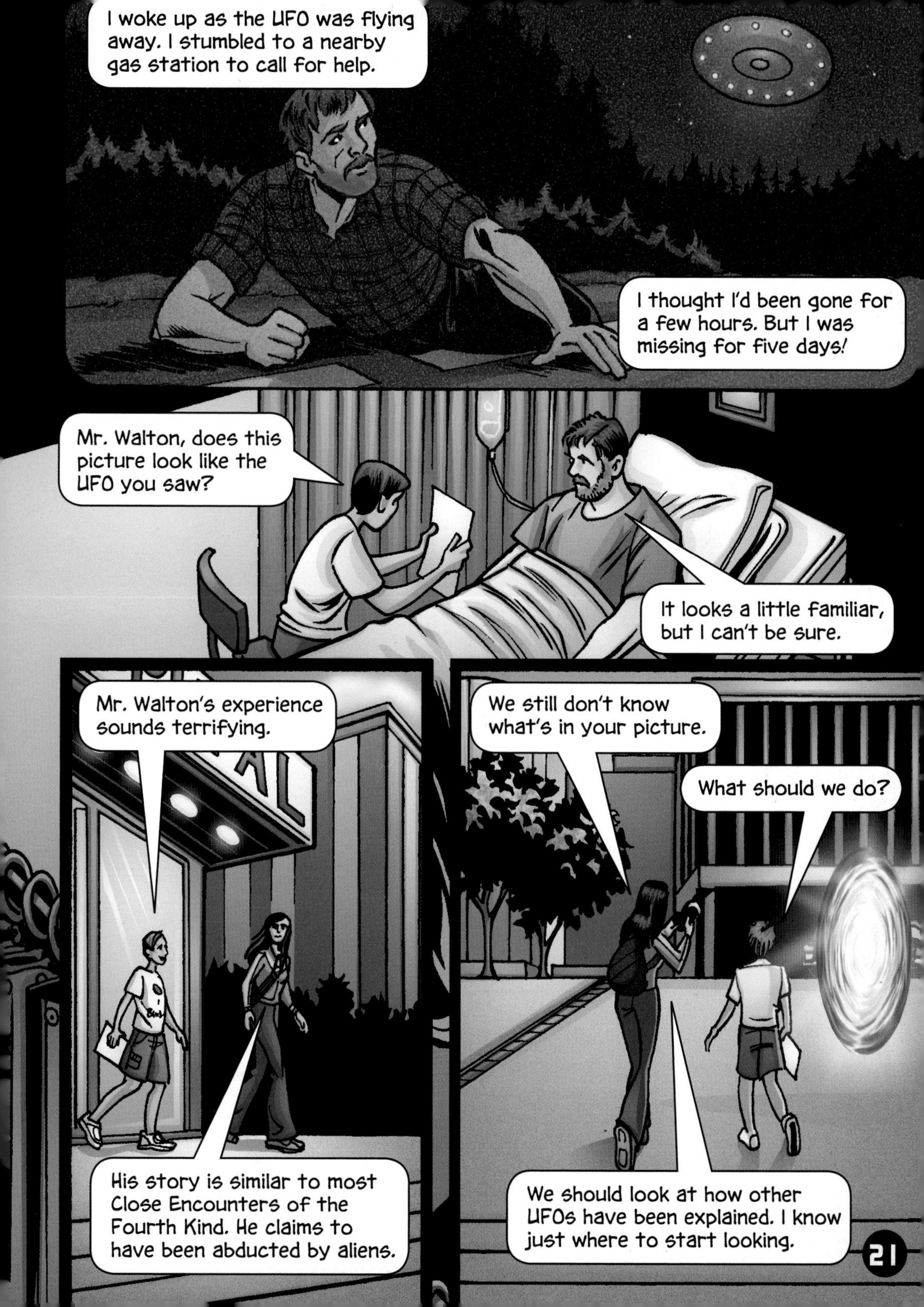
I woke up as the UFO was flying away. I stumbled to a nearby gas station to call for help.
I thought I'd been gone for a few hours. But I was missing for five days!
Mr. Walton, does this picture look like the UFO you saw?
It looks a little familiar, but I can't be sure.
Mr. Walton's experience sounds terrifying.
His story is similar to most Close Encounters of the Fourth Kind. He claims to have been abducted by aliens.
We still don't know what's in your picture.
What should we do?
We should look at how other UFOs have been explained. I know just where to start looking.

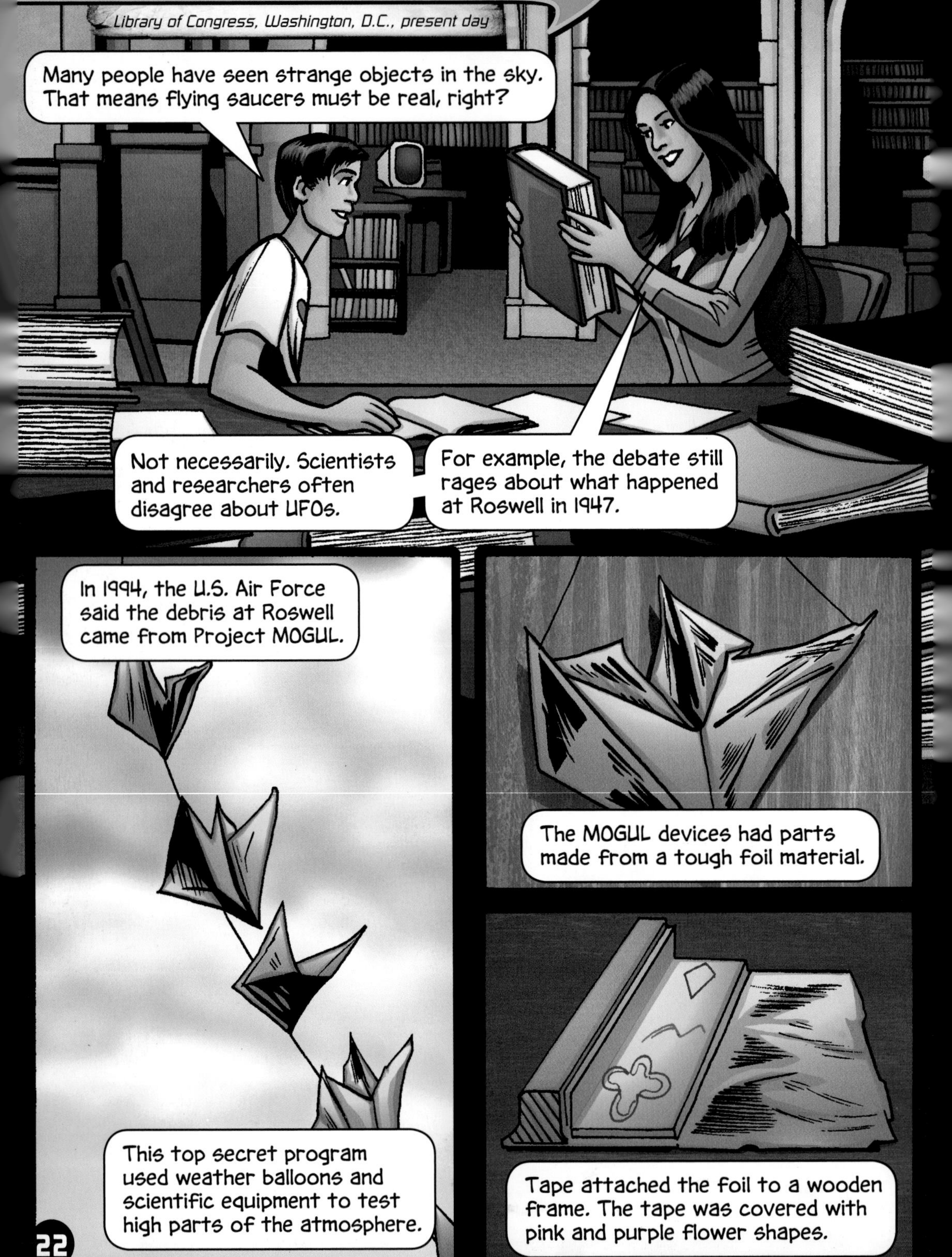
Library of Congress, Washington, D.C., present day
Many people have seen strange objects in the sky. That means flying saucers must be real, right?
Not necessarily. Scientists and researchers often disagree about UFOs.
For example, the debate still rages about what happened at Roswell in 1947.
In 1994, the U.S. Air Force said the debris at Roswell came from Project MOGUL.
This top secret program used weather balloons and scientific equipment to test high parts of the atmosphere.
The MOGUL devices had parts made from a tough foil material.
Tape attached the foil to a wooden frame. The tape was covered with pink and purple flower shapes.

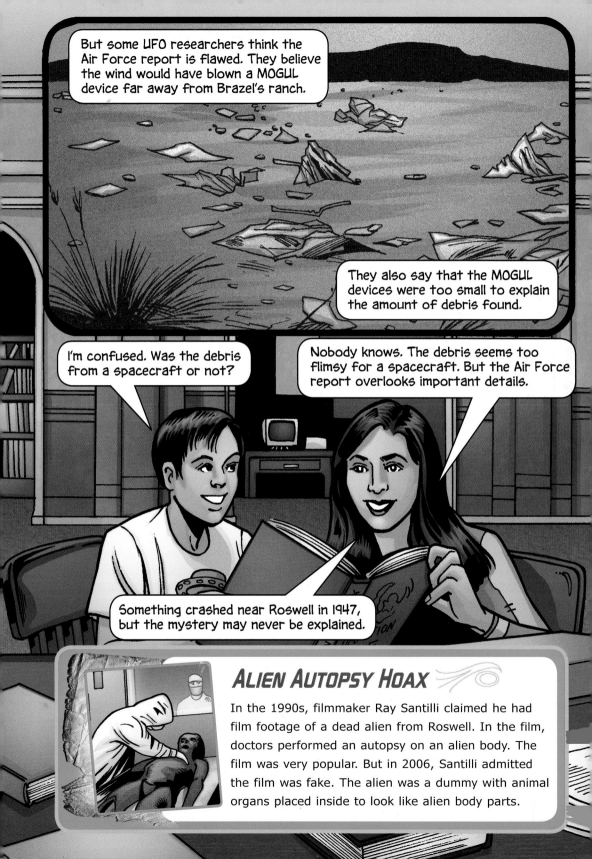

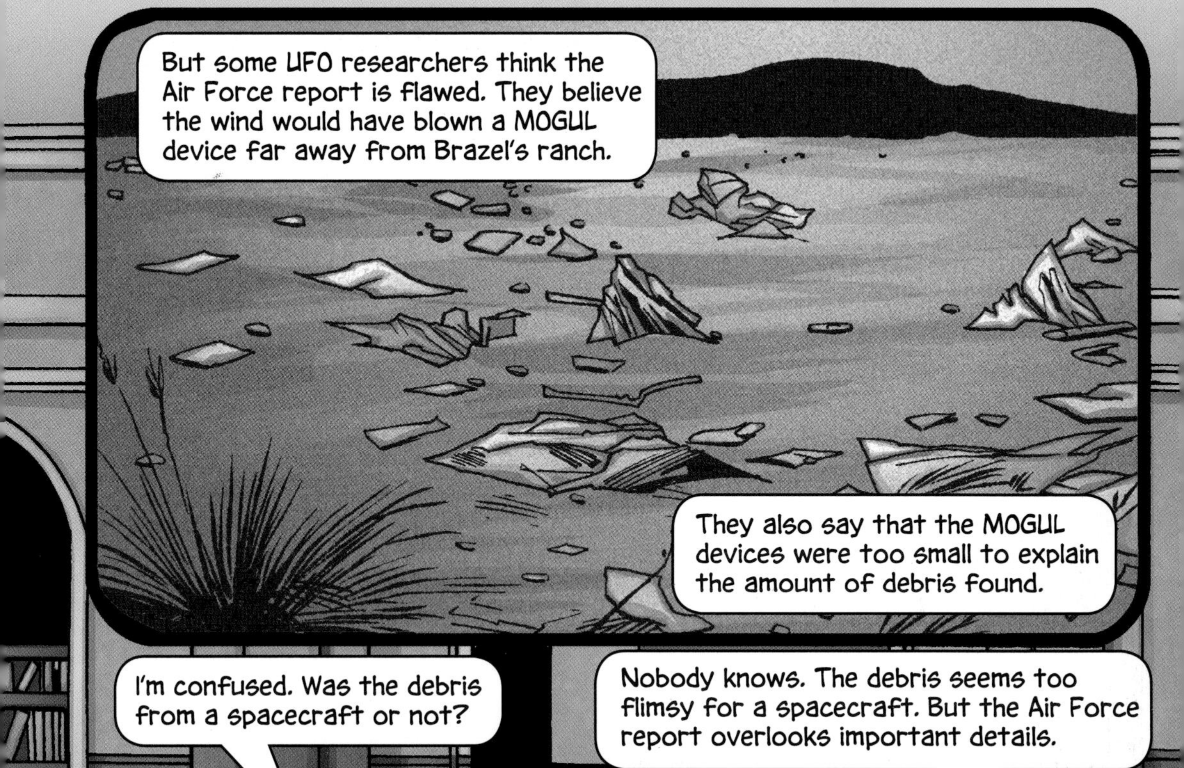
But some UFO researchers think the Air Force report is flawed. They believe the wind would have blown a MOGUL device far away from Brazel's ranch.
They also say that the MOGUL devices were too small to explain the amount of debris found.
I'm confused. Was the debris from a spacecraft or not?
Nobody knows. The debris seems too flimsy for a spacecraft. But the Air Force report overlooks important details.
Something crashed near Roswell in 1947, but the mystery may never be explained.

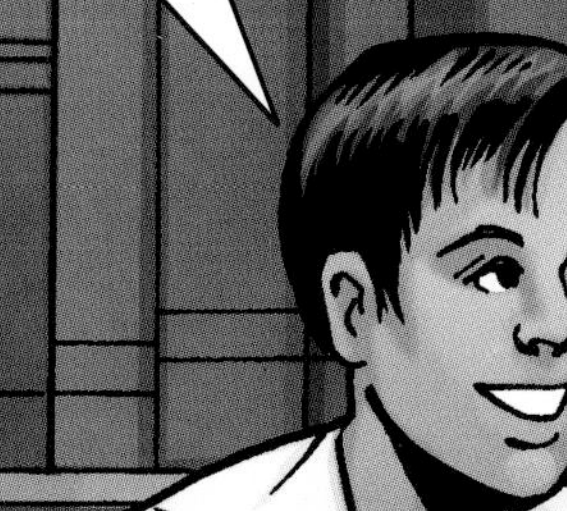

Alien Autopsy Hoax

In the 1990s, filmmaker Ray Santilli claimed he had film footage of a dead alien from Roswell. In the film, doctors performed an autopsy on an alien body. The film was very popular. But in 2006, Santilli admitted the film was fake. The alien was a dummy with animal organs placed inside to look like alien body parts.

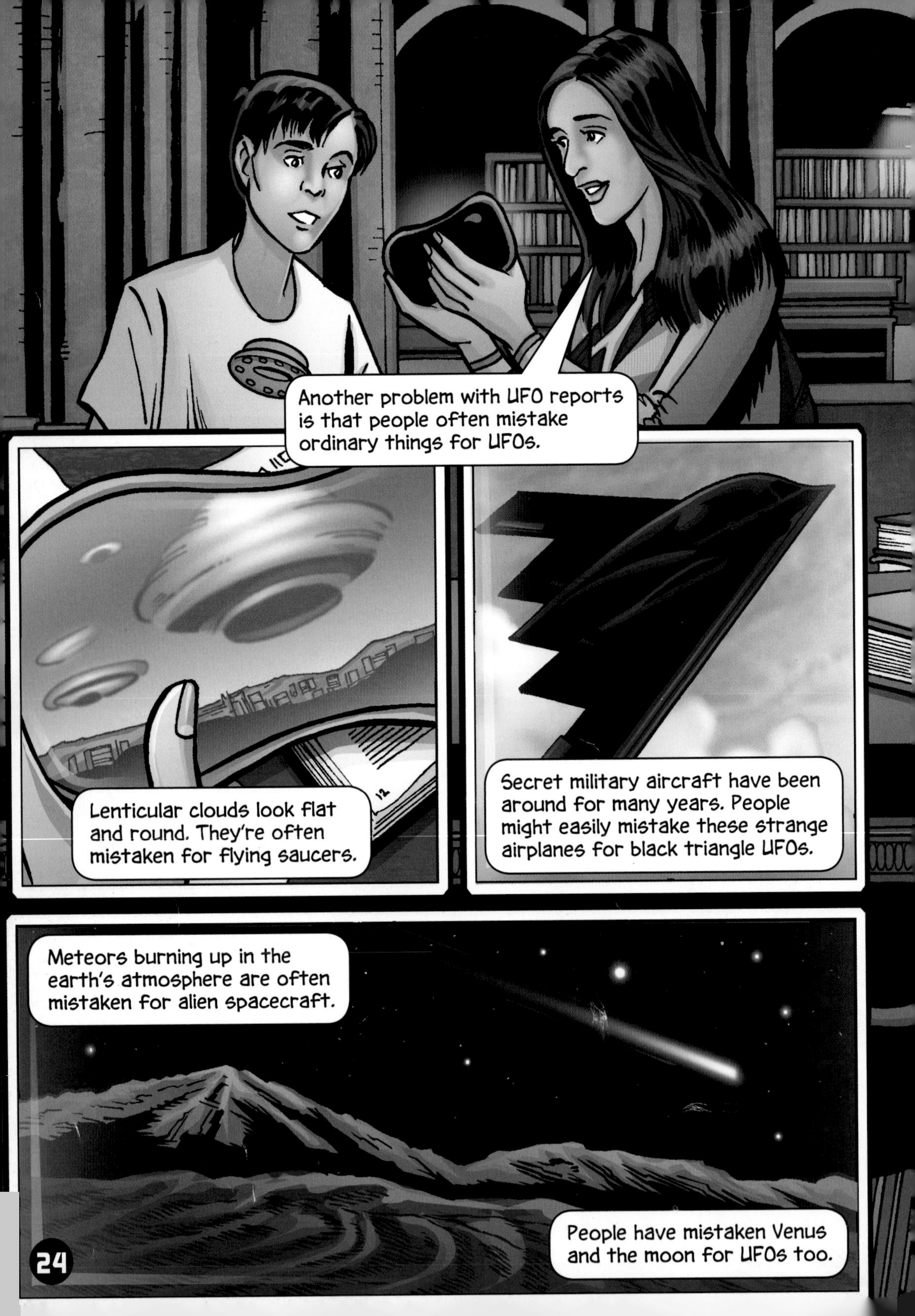
Another problem with UFO reports is that people often mistake ordinary things for UFOs.
Lenticular clouds look flat and round. They're often mistaken for flying saucers.
Secret military aircraft have been around for many years. People might easily mistake these strange airplanes for black triangle UFOs.
Meteors burning up in the earth's atmosphere are often mistaken for alien spacecraft.
People have mistaken Venus and the moon for UFOs too.

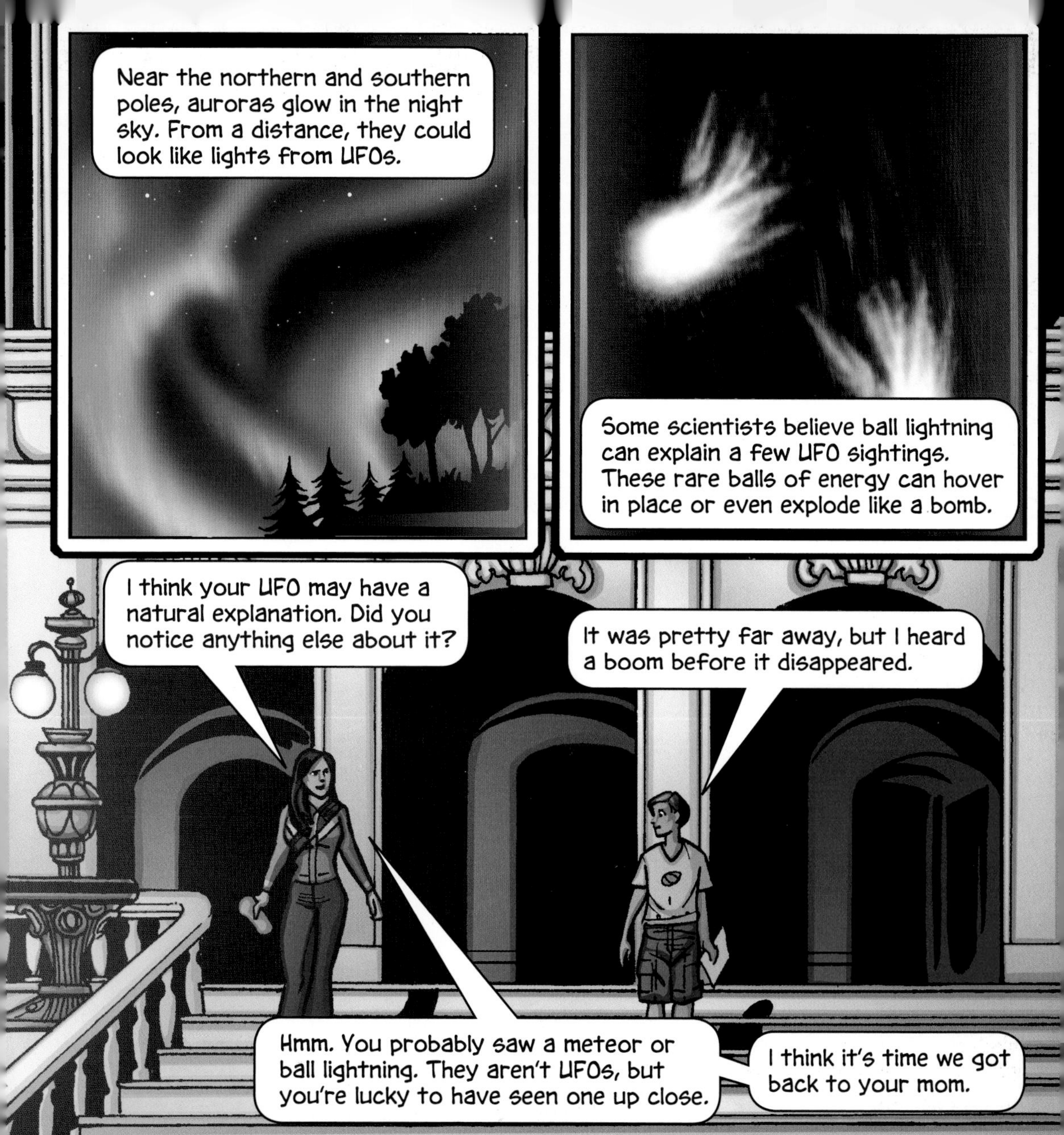
Near the northern and southern poles, auroras glow in the night sky. From a distance, they could look like lights from UFOs.
Some scientists believe ball lightning can explain a few UFO sightings. These rare balls of energy can hover in place or even explode like a bomb.
I think your UFO may have a natural explanation. Did you notice anything else about it?
It was pretty far away, but I heard a boom before it disappeared.
Hmm. You probably saw a meteor or ball lightning. They aren't UFOs, but you're lucky to have seen one up close.
I think it's time we got back to your mom.

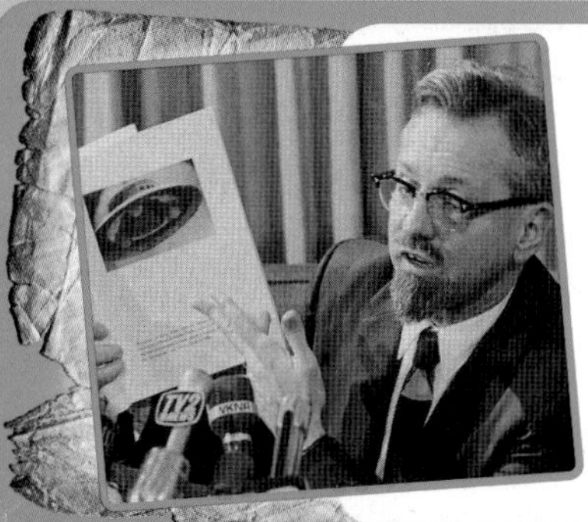

PROJECT BLUE BOOK

From 1952 to 1970, Project Blue Book investigated thousands of UFO sightings for the U.S. Air Force. This team of scientists wanted to find out if UFOs were real. They determined that most UFOs were either hoaxes or had logical explanations. However, a small number of UFO reports were unexplainable.

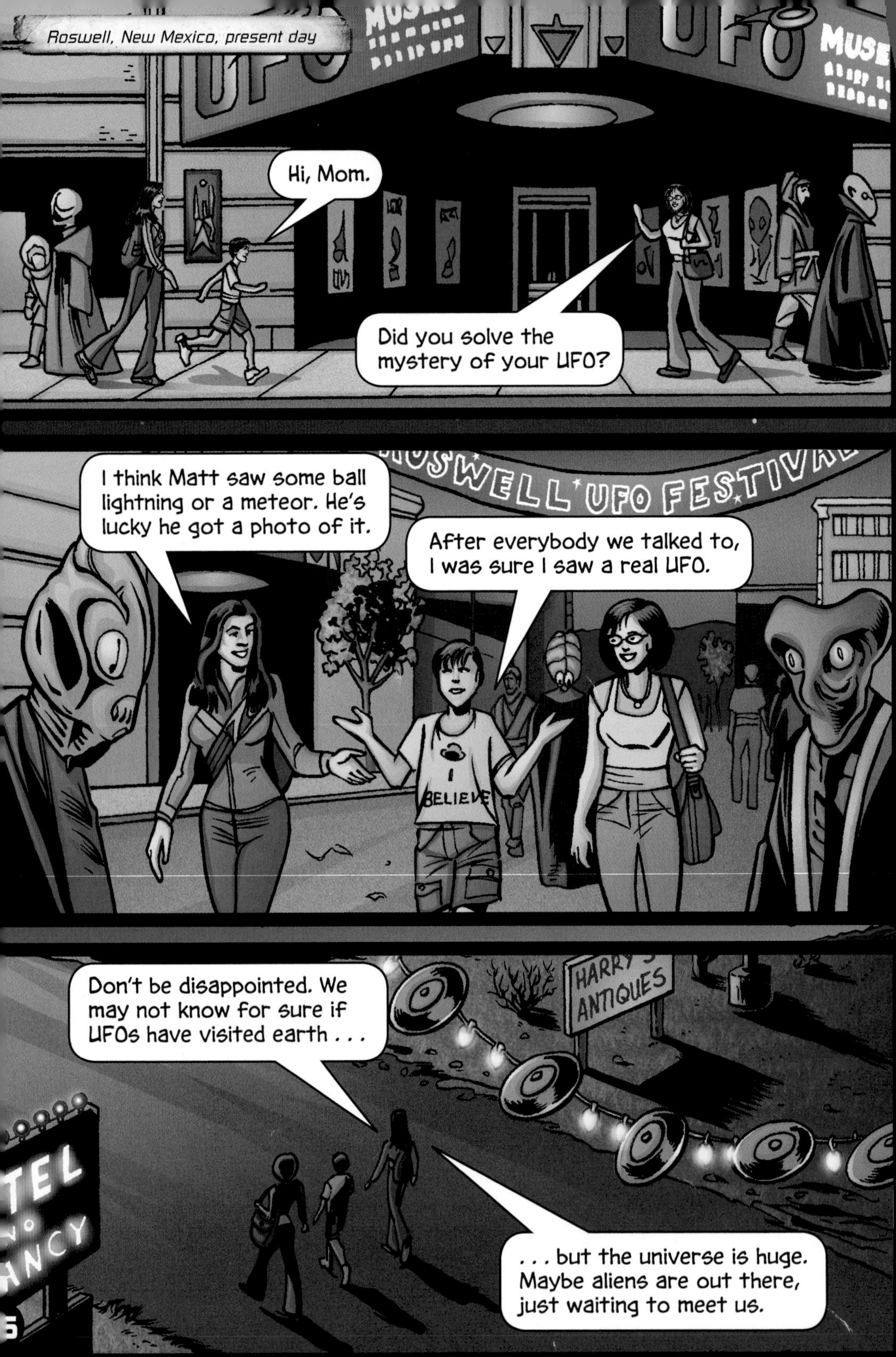
Roswell, New Mexico, present day
UFO MUSEUM
Hi, Mom.
Did you solve the mystery of your UFO?
ROSWELL UFO FESTIVAL
I think Matt saw some ball lightning or a meteor. He's lucky he got a photo of it.
After everybody we talked to, I was sure I saw a real UFO.
I BELIEVE
Don't be disappointed. We may not know for sure if UFOs have visited earth . . .
HARRY'S ANTIQUES
. . . but the universe is huge. Maybe aliens are out there, just waiting to meet us.

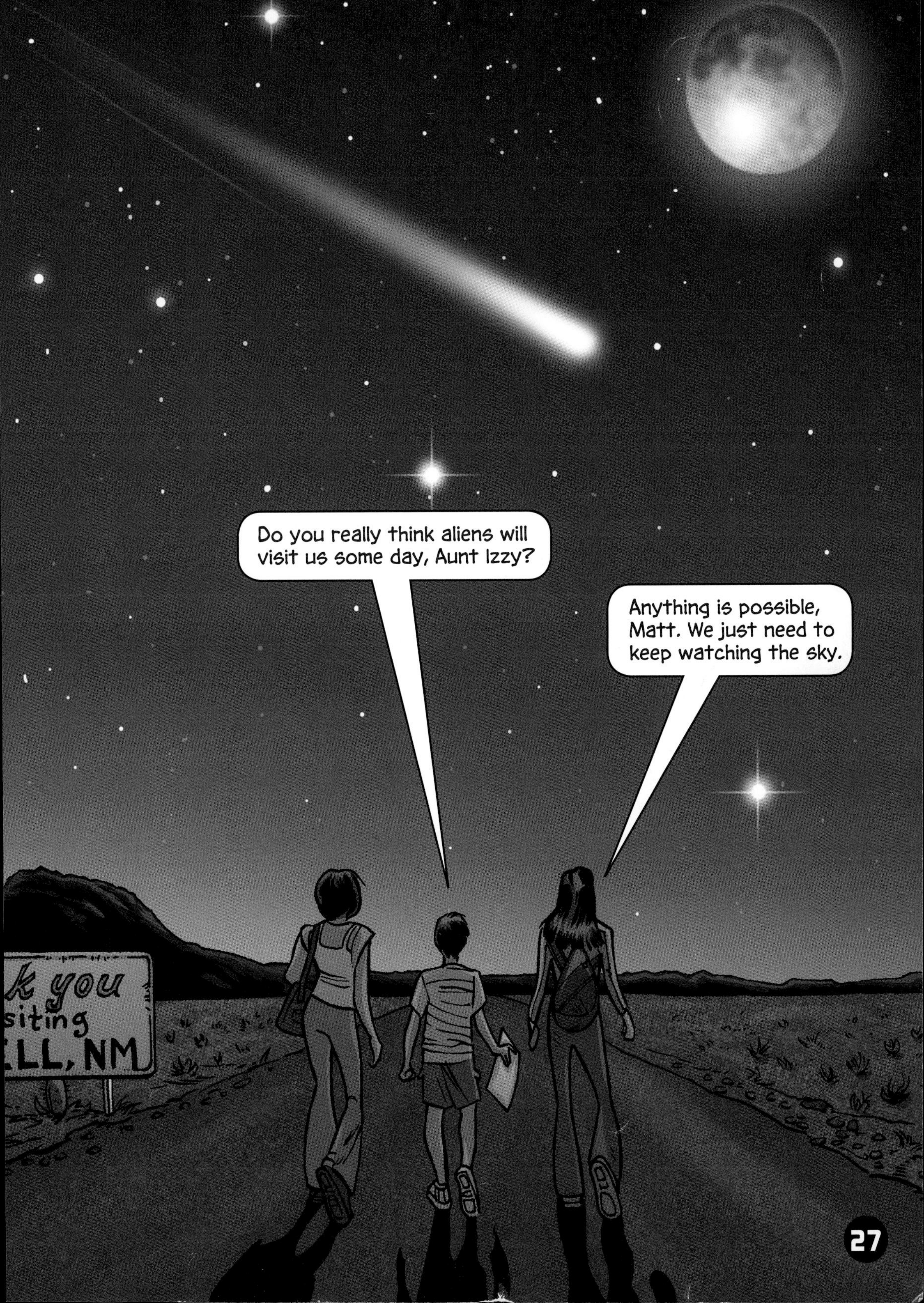
Do you really think aliens will visit us some day, Aunt Izzy?
Anything is possible, Matt. We just need to keep watching the sky.

MORE ABOUT UFOs

🌀 Several people claim Men in Black, or MIBs, visited them after UFO sightings. These men dress in black suits, black hats, and dark sunglasses. They claim to work for the government and usually threaten UFO witnesses if they talk about what they saw. Nobody knows if these mysterious men are real or not.

🌀 In 1938, Orson Welles broadcast a radio play of *The War of the Worlds*. Welles interrupted a regular radio show with news about Martians invading New York. The broadcast caused people to panic because they believed aliens had actually landed. The next day Welles and the radio station had to explain that the news announcement was part of the play.

🌀 People have claimed to see many kinds of aliens. The Grays are one of the most common. These short, hairless aliens have gray skin, large black eyes, and a small slit for a mouth. Nordic aliens look like humans. They are tall, muscular, and have blond hair and large blue or yellow eyes. Some alien sightings include small green, goblinlike creatures with bulging yellow eyes. Others have thick, wrinkly skin like an elephant.

🌀 The U.S. Air Force develops and tests secret experimental aircraft at Area 51 in Nevada. UFO sightings and other strange things are often reported near Area 51. Many people believe the U.S. government experiments with captured UFOs there.

- Since 1960, the Search for Extraterrestrial Intelligence Institute, or SETI, has been listening for alien radio signals. SETI scientists scan the stars with huge radio telescopes, hoping to hear signs of intelligent life. So far, SETI has only heard static.

- In March 1997, bright lights in a triangle formation were reported in Arizona. In Phoenix several people took photos and videos of the lights hovering over the city. The U.S. Air Force said the lights were flares from fighter planes. But thousands of people believe the lights were real UFOs.

MORE ABOUT

Isabel Soto

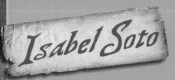

NAME: Dr. Isabel "Izzy" Soto
DEGREES: History and Anthropology
BUILD: Athletic **HAIR:** Dark Brown
EYES: Brown **HEIGHT:** 5′ 7″

W.I.S.P.: The Worldwide Inter-dimensional Space/Time Portal developed by Max Axiom at Axiom Laboratory.

BACKSTORY: Dr. Isabel "Izzy" Soto caught the history bug as a little girl. Every night, her grandfather told her about his adventures exploring ancient ruins in South America. He believed lost cultures teach people a great deal about history.

Izzy's love of cultures followed her to college. She studied history and anthropology. On a research trip to Thailand, she discovered an ancient stone with mysterious energy. Izzy took the stone to Super Scientist Max Axiom who determined that the stone's energy cuts across space and time. Harnessing the power of the stone, he built a device called the W.I.S.P. It opens windows to any place and any time. Izzy now travels through time to see history unfold before her eyes. Although she must not change history, she can observe and investigate historical events.

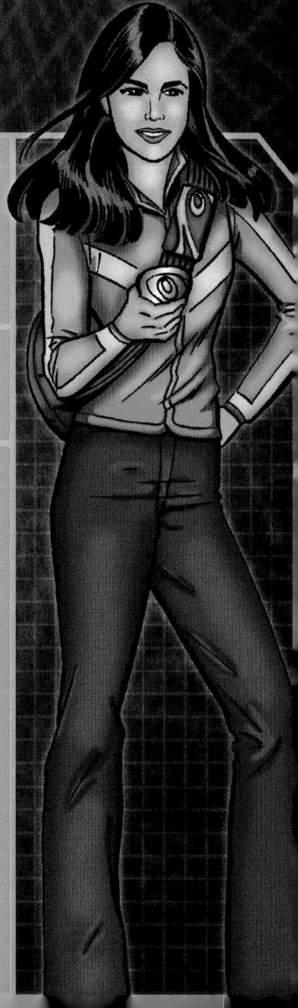

GLOSSARY

abduct (ab-DUKT) — to take someone away by force

atomic bomb (uh-TOM-ik BOM) — a bomb that splits atoms and explodes with great force; atomic bombs destroy large areas and leave behind dangerous radiation.

aurora (uh-ROHR-uh) — colorful bands of light; people can see auroras in the sky if they are far north or far south of the equator.

autopsy (AW-top-see) — a detailed study of a dead body to determine the cause and manner of death

close encounter (KLOHZ en-KOUN-tur) — an event where someone sees an unidentified flying object

debris (duh-BREE) — the scattered pieces of something that has been broken or destroyed

hieroglyph (HYE-ruh-glif) — a picture or symbol used in the ancient Egyptian system of writing

hoax (HOHKS) — a trick to make people believe something that is not true

incident (IN-suh-duhnt) — something that happens; an event.

meteor (MEE-tee-ur) — a piece of rock or dust that enters the earth's atmosphere, causing a streak of light in the sky

UFO (YOO EF OH) — an object in the sky thought to be a spaceship from another planet; UFO is short for unidentified flying object.

weather balloon (WETH-ur buh-LOON) — a balloon that carries instruments into the air to measure pressure, temperature, and other details about the atmosphere

READ MORE

Burns, Jan. *UFOs.* Mysterious Encounters. Detroit: KidHaven Press, 2008.

DeMolay, Jack. *UFOs: The Roswell Incident.* Jr. Graphic Mysteries. New York: PowerKids Press, 2007.

Grace, N. B. *UFOs: What Scientists Say May Shock You!* New York: Franklin Watts, 2008.

Jeffrey, Gary. *UFOs: Alien Abduction and Close Encounters.* Graphic Mysteries. New York: Rosen Central, 2006.

Nobleman, Marc Tyler. *Aliens and UFOs.* Atomic. Chicago: Raintree, 2007.

INTERNET SITES

FactHound offers a safe, fun way to find Internet sites related to this book. All sites on FactHound have been researched by our staff.

Here's all you do:

Visit *www.facthound.com*

FactHound will fetch the best sites for you!

INDEX